My Lai

WITNESS TO HISTORY

Peter Charles Hoffer and Williamjames Hoffer, *Series Editors*

ALSO IN THE SERIES:

Peter Charles Hoffer, *When Benjamin Franklin Met the Reverend Whitefield: Enlightenment, Revival, and the Power of the Printed Word*

Williamjames Hull Hoffer, *The Caning of Charles Sumner: Honor, Idealism, and the Origins of the Civil War*

Tim Lehman, *Bloodshed at Little Bighorn: Sitting Bull, Custer, and the Destinies of Nations*

Daniel R. Mandell, *King Philip's War: Colonial Expansion, Native Resistance, and the End of Indian Sovereignty*

Erik R. Seeman, *The Huron-Wendat Feast of the Dead: Indian-European Encounters in Early North America*

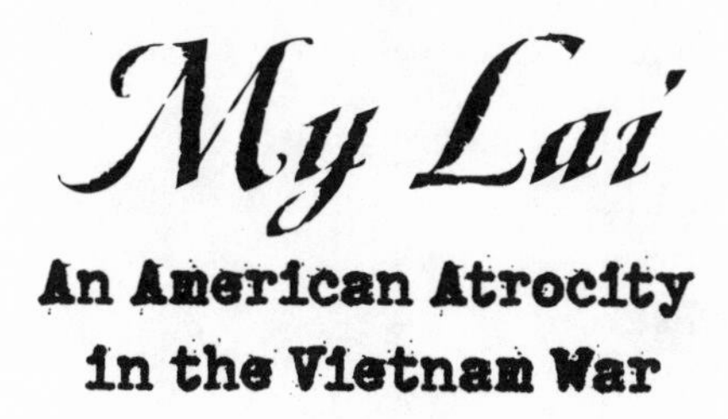

WILLIAM THOMAS ALLISON

The Johns Hopkins University Press | *Baltimore*

© 2012 The Johns Hopkins University Press
All rights reserved. Published 2012
Printed in the United States of America on acid-free paper
9 8 7 6 5 4 3 2 1

The Johns Hopkins University Press
2715 North Charles Street
Baltimore, Maryland 21218-4363
www.press.jhu.edu

Library of Congress Cataloging-in-Publication Data

Allison, William Thomas.
My Lai : an American atrocity in the Vietnam War / William Thomas Allison.
p. cm. — (Witness to history)
Includes bibliographical references and index.
ISBN 978-1-4214-0644-2 (hdbk. : acid-free paper) — ISBN 978-1-4214-0645-9 (pbk. : acid-free paper) — ISBN 978-1-4214-0706-7 (electronic) — ISBN 1-4214-0644-6 (hdbk. : acid-free paper) — ISBN 1-4214-0645-4 (pbk. : acid-free paper) — ISBN 1-4214-0706-X (electronic)
1. My Lai Massacre, Vietnam, 1968. 2. Vietnam War, 1961–1975—Atrocities. I. Title.
DS557.8.M9A44 2012
959.704'342—dc23 2011053280

A catalog record for this book is available from the British Library.

Special discounts are available for bulk purchases of this book. For more information, please contact Special Sales at 410-516-6936 or specialsales@press.jhu.edu.

The Johns Hopkins University Press uses environmentally friendly book materials, including recycled text paper that is composed of at least 30 percent post-consumer waste, whenever possible.

War loves to seek its victims in the young.

Sophocles

CONTENTS

My Lai

Prologue

> Only the nation that has faced up to its own failings and acknowledged its capacities for evil and ill-doing has any real claim to greatness.
>
> Time, *December 5, 1969*

On March 16, 1968, soldiers of Task Force Barker killed as many as five hundred Vietnamese men, women, and children in a village complex in Quang Ngai Province called Son My. Of these soldiers, several from Charlie Company, 1st Battalion, 11th Infantry, committed most of the killing in a hamlet identified on American maps as My Lai (4), known to Vietnamese as Xom Lang. The incident remained something of a secret for almost a year. Once revealed, it spawned investigations that implicated dozens of soldiers and officers in the killing and/or subsequent cover-up. Of these, however, only a handful ultimately stood before a court-martial, with only one convicted of any wrongdoing.

My Lai provided a lightning rod to channel the highly charged voices both of those who opposed the American war in Vietnam and those who supported it. Although the incident happened in 1968, its place in that remarkable year of years eludes definition because the American public did not learn of the massacre until 1969, from which point it remained in the near constant forefront of the American media until the trials ended in 1974. Think of all that occurred in the United States in the interim: Martin Luther King, Jr., and Robert Kennedy were assassinated; Abbie Hoffman and the Yippies did their anarchic best to disrupt the National Democratic Party Convention in Chicago; Richard Nixon was elected president; the "Miracle Mets" won the World Series; Neil Armstrong walked on the moon; the world had to learn to live without the Beatles; Nixon was reelected; the American war in Vietnam ended; and the Watergate scandal forced Nixon to resign. The investigations and trials occurred amid antiwar protests, the drawdown of American forces from Vietnam, the deterioration of discipline and morale in the American military, and, among the American people, an increasing dissatisfaction with and distrust of the US government, including its military.

Fixed in the Vietnam generation's memory as the My Lai Massacre, it evokes uneasy emotions among Vietnamese and Americans old enough to remember the first news of the incident, the numerous inquiries, and the courts-martial, particularly that of Lieutenant William L. Calley, Jr. As the Vietnam generation begins to fade, however, so too does the collective memory of the Vietnam War and My Lai. Recent generations may have learned of My Lai, perhaps from a brief paragraph in an American history textbook, but increasingly, it seems, students in history classrooms have not. The purpose of this book is to offer students a concise but thorough overview of the context, events, legacies, and principal sources related to this horrific tragedy in the hope of making them aware so that they, too, will remember.

When studying My Lai, students should be mindful of the problems associated with finding the "truth" about what really happened in this and similar events. Like the several witnesses of a proverbial car wreck, none of whom saw exactly the same thing, so too with My Lai. Even as the killing unfolded the morning of March 16, 1968, no one initially had any idea of the totality of what was happening. No one person saw everything that happened. Even witnesses of the same incident remember different things about what they saw. Moreover, soldiers' memories faded and stories intentionally and unintentionally changed over the many months before investigators from the Army Criminal Investigation Division (CID) and the Peers Inquiry interviewed them. Additionally, the role played by some of those who were not physically present at My Lai that morning remains unclear. While few today contest that a cover-up occurred, showing any level of conspiracy to hide the incident is nonetheless difficult.

The approach I have taken in this book is to aid the reader in dissecting the principal events surrounding My Lai. The book is not intended to be definitive, but rather, by pulling together materials from the investigations and trials with scholarship on My Lai, the Vietnam War, and other related issues, it gives readers a detailed overview of My Lai. Students can then place the event in the overall context of American history to glean both historical and contemporary insights and pursue further inquiry.

Atrocities, alleged and proven, committed by American forces in the Iraq and Afghanistan wars give more than enough reason to remember and learn from My Lai. To deny My Lai's relevance is to deny the past and any role that history may play in a nation's growth, memory, and being. History, unfortunately, provides a litany of tragic examples of atrocity committed by a military force upon noncombatants of differing race and ethnicity. In the American experience, one can look to such incidents as the tragic massacres of Native Americans at Sand Creek or Wounded Knee in the nineteenth century, both instructive in their own right, but My Lai holds particular resonance because of the time in which it occurred. Vietnam, the Cold War, the 1960s, the antiwar movement, counterculture, the rage of antiauthority among American youth—these and other events and trends engulfing the United States and much of the world during this painfully exciting era intrigue Americans in both a nostalgic and haunting way that continues to fascinate scholars and commentators alike.

War is an uncivilized activity that over time humans have attempted to refine through custom, law, and convention. Despite these attempts, combatants have committed and will continue to commit atrocities against each other and noncombatants. Americans in particular do not like to think that their sons and daughters are capable of brutality akin to that committed by Nazi SS forces or the Japanese Imperial Army during World War II. But as My Lai revealed during the Vietnam War and isolated incidents in the recent wars in Iraq and Afghanistan have shown, Americans are capable of violent military atrocity. Like good, evil too is a human condition. While engrossed in the good its people can offer broader humanity, a great nation must also understand, as best it can, its people's capacity for evil.

1 Charlie Company and Vietnam

Our mission was not to win terrain or seize positions, but simply to kill: to kill Communists and to kill as many of them as possible. Stack 'em like cordwood.

Philip Caputo, A Rumor of War

WHEN THE TRAGIC EVENTS occurred at My Lai on March 16, 1968, the American war in Vietnam had already taken a dramatic turn.[1] By 1967, the United States had become fully embroiled in a dual effort both to stabilize the South Vietnamese government and economy and to destroy the Viet Cong (VC) insurgency in the countryside while carrying out a more conventional fight against the North Vietnamese Army (NVA) near the Demilitarized Zone (DMZ) and bombing targets in North Vietnam. Late that same year, General William C. Westmoreland, commander of the US Military Assistance Command, Vietnam (MACV), claimed that the war of attrition in South Vietnam approached a crossover point in favor of an American–South Vietnamese victory, telling the National Press Club in Washington, DC, "I am absolutely certain that whereas in 1965 the enemy was winning, today he is certainly losing."[2] Despite these positive pronouncements, the American economy shuddered against the increasing financial burden of the conflict, coinciding with growing public protest against the human cost of the war. President Lyndon Johnson's approval ratings began to slide. With almost 500,000 troops in

Vietnam and over 19,000 Americans killed in the conflict through 1967, the American people wanted either to see real progress or to get out.

On the night of January 30, 1968, the Tet New Year, Viet Cong units staged attacks across South Vietnam, hitting provincial capitals, major cities, and military installations. In Saigon, Viet Cong advance units that had earlier infiltrated the city attacked the Presidential Palace, radio station, and, most symbolically damaging for the United States, the American Embassy. Unfortunately for the Viet Cong, NVA and other Viet Cong units failed in their follow-up attacks, while American and South Vietnamese forces quickly recovered to overwhelm the assaults, bloodying the Viet Cong in the process. Except for extended fighting in the Cholon District of Saigon and the old imperial city of Hue, the initial phase of the Tet Offensive ended in a week's time. The North Vietnamese siege of the American base at Khe Sanh in northwestern South Vietnam, thought by Westmoreland to be the main target of the offensive, lasted well into March before the North Vietnamese withdrew. Thousands of civilians and South Vietnamese troops had been killed, as had hundreds of American soldiers and Marines.

In the United States, television news showed dead American soldiers near the American Embassy, the execution of a suspected Viet Cong by the commander of South Vietnam's national police, and the intense house-to-house fighting in Hue, among other gritty images. The Tet Offensive was a shock to the American war effort and it made illegitimate the gains previously claimed by Westmoreland and the Johnson administration. Although a military defeat for the Viet Cong and a serious setback for the North Vietnamese, Tet proved politically less damaging for both. As the American public asked more questions about the war, President Johnson decided in March not to seek reelection and reversed American strategy in Vietnam, all but publically admitting that the United States could not win the war.

The American Combat Experience in Vietnam

Other than a comparatively limited number of major actions, such as Operation Cedar Falls and the battles of Khe Sanh, Hue, and An Loc, brief but lethal engagements involving platoon- to company-sized units characterized infantry combat in Vietnam.[3] Even then, an American soldier had just as much a chance of being killed or wounded by a mine or booby trap without actually seeing the enemy. The American military had been equipped, manned, and trained to fight a big-unit war in Western Europe against similarly styled Soviet forces, resulting in a heavy American force doctrinally dependent upon technology and massive firepower. Arguably ill suited for fighting in Vietnam, the American military faced an experienced enemy versed in both guerrilla tactics and conventional capabilities.

Moreover, many younger Americans in the early 1960s had a skewed perception of war. Hollywood movies portrayed to American youth a John Wayne who had heroically won World War II then returned home a completely well-adjusted hero. Their fathers and grandfathers told them how great armies had invaded Normandy and landed on Iwo Jima, fighting an enemy clearly distinguished in both appearance and character, to achieve clearly defined objectives in an unconditional victory. Young boys played war World War II–style. This perception of the Second World War, which survived the Korean War, firmly embedded the glory of war and American self-righteousness in American culture and conscience. Philip Caputo, who served as a young Marine officer in Vietnam in 1965–66, recalled his expectations of war: "I saw myself charging up some distant beachhead, like John Wayne in *Sands of Iwo Jima*, and then coming home with medals on my chest."[4] While such misguided beliefs may have motivated young men to enlist in military service in the early 1960s, they certainly shaped in them a very false expectation of the nature of war in Southeast Asia.

Vietnam failed to fit this popularly accepted rubric of war. The Viet Cong did not wear uniforms. Nor did they respect traditional battle lines, which did not exist in the guerrilla war the Viet Cong waged in the south, forcing MACV to declare the entire country of South Vietnam a combat zone. The enemy seemed elusive and not as easily identified as in wars past, while the local people seemed ungrateful compared to the joyous Europeans liberated by Allied forces in the Second World War. Like World War II and Korea, the war in Vietnam saw horrific carnage, suffering, and death, and as in those wars the American public knew little about the realities of the war in Vietnam. The grainy televised scenes of death and destruction during the Tet Offensive gave the American public its first deep immersion into the real Vietnam. In their book *Four Hours in My Lai*, Michael Bilton and Kevin Sim rightly asserted that in Vietnam "an army with its head in the clouds had been sent to war by a nation with its head in the sand." For the many soldiers and veterans disillusioned by the realities of the war in Vietnam, "Fuck you, John Wayne" became their mantra.[5]

The military force the United States sent to Vietnam reflected President Johnson's refusal to mobilize the reserves for service in Southeast Asia. Worried that full mobilization would antagonize China and the Soviet Union and anxious about domestic political and economic implications of calling up the reserves, Johnson relied upon Selective Service, commonly known as the draft, to provide soldiers for service in Vietnam. Unlike the Marines, the Air Force, and the Navy, which relied mostly upon volunteers, the Army turned to the draft, and the threat of being drafted, to fulfill its personnel needs.

As the Johnson administration escalated the number of troops in Vietnam, drafted inductees dramatically increased from 120,000 in fiscal year 1965, to over 320,000 for fiscal year 1966, to 334,000 in fiscal year 1967. Controversy surrounded the draft process, as numerous deferments—such as working a defense-related job, being married, serving in the National Guard, or attending college—as well as the inconsistencies presented by over 4,000 local draft boards, often favored the affluent at the expense of the working class among American youth. The burden of service, therefore, largely fell upon young working-class Americans, African Americans in particular, who could not afford to enroll in college or otherwise get a deferment.

The typical draftee was nevertheless both younger and better educated compared to his World War II counterpart. So, too, was the typical enlistee, or volunteer. The average age of the American soldier in World War II had been twenty-six; in Vietnam, the average age barely reached nineteen. Twenty-four percent of the World War II Army had completed high school and just over 13 percent had attended college. In the Vietnam Army, almost 80 percent had graduated from high school and 30 percent of enlisted personnel (sergeant, or E-5, and below) had attended college. Still, lack of education made it more likely one would be sent to Vietnam once in the military, as enlisted personnel who had dropped out of high school had a 70 percent chance of being deployed to Vietnam, compared to 60 percent for high school graduates and 42 percent for college graduates. Moreover, the less education, the more likely a soldier would see combat in Vietnam.[6]

The draft motivated many to volunteer under the pretext that enlistees had a better chance than draftees of getting noncombat assignments. A draftee, for example, was two times more likely to be killed in Vietnam than was an enlistee. In 1968, 54 percent of enlistees admitted draft motivation, as did 60 percent of officers and 80 percent of reservists. From 1964 to 1973, when the draft ended, the draft took 2.2 million American men, compared to the 8.7 million who enlisted. As a point of comparison, over 16 million males of draft age did not see military service during the Vietnam era.

During the early years of American escalation, the Army mostly had volunteers in Vietnam. With the demand for more troops, however, by 1969 draftees made up over 88 percent of infantrymen in Vietnam. This rapid expansion required more junior officers and noncommissioned officers (NCOs) that the reserves might otherwise have provided. The Army also faced the problem of training thousands of draftees with NCOs and junior officers while needing those very same trainers for duty in Vietnam. To supply these much-needed officers and NCOs, the Army turned to accelerated commissioning and training programs. Whereas prior to Vietnam the Army could rely upon West Point and Reserve Officer Training Corps (ROTC) programs at colleges and universities to commission second lieutenants, beginning in 1965 the vast majority of junior officers would be commissioned through Officer Candidate School (OCS), which similarly had produced most of the junior officers during World War II. This system had worked before; few saw any reason why it should not work again.

For NCOs, the Army compressed the normal five years it took for a worthy private to advance to sergeant by giving two-grade promotions in the field, advancing an E-3 (private first-class, or PFC) to E-5 to provide much-needed squad leaders in Vietnam. Additionally, in 1967 the Army began offering a twelve-week Noncommissioned Officer Candidate program to enlisted personnel upon completion of basic training. By 1968, this "shake and bake" process produced over 13,000 NCOs. A typical infantry company in this "Vietnam only" Army, then, might include one or two senior NCOs and regular Army lieutenants, but the majority came from shake and bake programs and OCS. Enlisted personnel were mostly draftees or single-term enlistees.

Regardless of one's status as an officer, NCO, or enlisted person, the organizing concept of a soldier's life in Vietnam centered on the twelve-month tour of duty (thirteen months for Marines), one of the more controversial features of the American approach to fighting in Vietnam. While some attributed the low rate of psychiatric injuries among American troops (6 percent in Vietnam compared to 23 percent during World War II) as the principal benefit of the twelve-month system, others pointed to the negative disruption of units the system caused, as personnel rotated in and out on a near weekly basis. Such conditions made unit cohesion difficult with a constant influx of "fucking new guys" (FNGs), who required additional orientation and training. Ideally, a soldier needed at least six months to gain the experience necessary to be effective in combat. Under the twelve-month tour policy a soldier might have four months effectiveness before "short-timer's syndrome" took over and made him less so as his "date eligible for return from overseas" (DEROS) approached. Every soldier knew his DEROS. Despite concerns voiced by many of his subordinates, Westmoreland, who conceived of the twelve-month tour concept, stubbornly continued the policy throughout his tenure as commander of MACV.

For officers, the standard tour included six months in the field plus six months in a staff position in country. Consequently, the Army took an officer off the line just when he ideally became effective. The few proponents of the six-month period in the field argued that after six months field officers suffer from exhaustion and begin to make poor decisions. Many more officers, however, rejected this notion, arguing instead that just when they got the hang of commanding in the field, their time expired, resulting in companies and platoons becoming training units for inexperienced officers rather than operating as veteran fighting units. Careerism also played a role, as officers at all levels could get both combat and staff experience in twelve months, then rotate to other assignments. This "ticket punching" did little for the morale of enlisted men struggling to survive twelve months in the field. As John Paul Vann, a seasoned Vietnam hand in both combat and pacification, apparently quipped, "We don't have twelve years' experience in Vietnam. We have one year's experience twelve times over."[7]

General Westmoreland used this force to fight a war of attrition against Viet Cong and NVA forces in South Vietnam. A strategy of attrition using American firepower, he reasoned, might bring victory sooner than a much longer-term strategy centered upon traditional counterinsurgency methods. Ultimately, the United States ineffectively pursued both strategies in Vietnam. Along with pacification programs, strategic hamlets, and other kinetic counterinsurgency operations, Westmoreland's planners utilized conventional firepower to grind down Viet Cong forces in South Vietnam. To achieve this attrition, the Army saw little need to capture and maintain control over large swaths of territory. Rather, attrition would come about through luring Viet Cong into the open, where lethal firepower—in the form of artillery from isolated firebases as well as airstrikes delivered by aircraft ranging from helicopters only hundreds of feet in the air to Arc Light strikes from B-52 bombers flying at 30,000 feet—would destroy the enemy. Eventually, the strategy held, the ratio of enemy losses to those suffered by friendly forces would reach a "crossover point," indicating the moment at which the enemy could no longer replace its losses. Additionally, in fighting a limited war, the Johnson administration's political decision against a conventional invasion of North Vietnam denied the Army and Marines the opportunity to capitalize on massive American firepower and advanced technology to destroy North Vietnamese and Viet Cong forces in a classic decisive battle of annihilation; the strategy of attrition thus arose almost by default.

To get the Viet Cong into the open, the Americans relied principally upon company- and platoon-sized patrols of Army, Marine, and ARVN (Army of the Republic of Vietnam) troops operating from firebases or transported by helicopter to make contact with the enemy, whereupon troops in the field would call in artillery or airstrikes to rain devastation on enemy forces. Other tactics included "search and destroy" operations, the objective of which involved not only the destruction of Viet Cong forces but also anything the Viet Cong could use for food, shelter, or transport. In either instance, the Army and Marines would often warn civilians of the impending operation and urge them to move to relocation camps, a nearby strategic hamlet, or other secure area, in order to minimize possible civilian casualties. In many cases, however, MACV simply designated large swaths of South Vietnam as "free-fire zones," in which entire areas would be laid to waste by carpet bombing. Patrols considered any Vietnamese civilians found within a free-fire zone to be enemy combatants. Other tactics included the use of chemical defoliants, such as the popularly known Agent Orange, to kill vegetation in order to rob the Viet Cong of cover. Ideally, Westmoreland wanted to destroy large Viet Cong and NVA units in decisive engagements. These units, however, understood the lethality of American firepower and therefore proved most reluctant to get caught in the open. When the enemy did mass in the open, such as during the Tet Offensive, American firepower was highly effective.

Fighting an insurgency with mostly conventional methods yielded little progress. Focused so much on destroying the enemy through attrition, Westmoreland neglected a basic principle of counterinsurgency—providing security for the people in the countryside so that they could in turn feel safe to rebuild their lives after so many years at war. Security would also bring stable government, which could then evolve into one made legitimate by the Vietnamese people. Deep corruption, however, infected everything from the national government down to local villages, a situation that made establishing legitimate authority difficult. Because MACV did not occupy and secure the countryside, American and South Vietnamese forces frequently had to revisit areas to root out returning Viet Cong. Such problems hindered progress in rural areas, including such places like Son My in Quang Ngai Province.

To measure the progress of attrition, Westmoreland and MACV relied upon tallying Viet Cong and NVA killed in action (KIA), literally referred to as a "body count" by the American military. Planners determined that the crossover point could be reached so long as the Americans and South Vietnamese maintained a ratio of ten enemy combatants killed to every one allied soldier lost. As the supreme measure of success, the body count blinded some commanders against employing alternative strategies and tactics more vigorously in South Vietnam, as they planned and carried out operations designed solely to maximize the number of enemy killed. For an ambitious officer, high body counts meant promotion and new command opportunities. Many commanders even gave prizes such as extra beer rations and three-day passes to units that reported the highest number of confirmed kills during an operation. Such incentives invited widespread inflation of body counts by as much as 30 percent and encouraged troops on the ground to play loose with rules of engagement (ROE) designed to protect noncombatants. A "shoot first, ask questions later" mentality infected commanders in the field who felt pressured by their superiors to exceed ambitious quotas.

In the midst of this strategy of attrition, American soldiers found themselves in a strange land of strange people. Vietnam's geography could easily overwhelm the senses of an American soldier, especially one from the Midwest, Great Plains, or arid West. Many found Vietnam a beautiful country, especially the pristine white sands of the coastal beaches and the intense greens of the triple canopy jungle, rice fields, and rubber plantations. Though rugged, the highlands of central Vietnam also held their own unique beauty. The heat, extreme humidity, and torrential rains during the monsoon season, however, made every aspect of an American soldier's life difficult. The red soil choked the lungs with dust during the dry months and turned to thick, sticky mud during the rainy season—whether dry or wet, it covered soldier and machine alike. Trench foot and "crotch rot" became the bane of the soldier's existence. Fever, "the trots," exposure to bug spray and defoliants, and a host of other maladies consistently lessened the fighting strength of any unit. Viet Cong booby traps could sometimes be the least of one's worries, as leeches, poisonous snakes, biting insects, and other menacing creatures added yet another element of danger to what on the surface appeared a peaceful preserve of unspoiled nature.

The culture also overwhelmed young American soldiers, who found the language, living conditions, and social behavior of the Vietnamese difficult to tolerate, much less to understand. Dehumanizing both the enemy and the people as "gooks," "slopes," or "dinks," much as their predecessors had in the Korean War, the Pacific war against Japan, and even earlier in the Philippines at the turn of the century, American troops frequently used these racist epithets for all Vietnamese, friend or foe. The enemy they faced mined and booby-trapped roads, trails, and hootches (rural Vietnamese homes or quarters for American personnel). Patrols found enemy tunnels and bunkers in almost every village and often lost troops to mines and snipers without engaging or even seeing any Viet Cong. Frustrated, many soldiers came to believe that local villagers knew the location of mines and booby traps but allowed the Americans to walk right into them. Widespread racial prejudice and the intense pressure to produce high body counts resulted in the "mere gook rule," which placed a Vietnamese at the bottom of the hierarchy of life in Vietnam. A 1966 survey of Marines then operating in Quang Ngai Province, for example, found that 40 percent strongly disliked the Vietnamese. Incidents of mistreatment of women, violent assault against and killing of Vietnamese, and pedestrian injuries and deaths involving American vehicles increased steadily from 1965 through 1970.

Such conditions perhaps made atrocities inevitable. "Humping" through the bush, jungle, and rice paddies, in energy-sapping heat and humidity and in torrential rain, not knowing when contact with an elusive enemy would occur, American troops experienced extreme levels of frustration and anxiety. Seeing their buddies killed or maimed by mines and booby traps in a place where women and children sometimes tossed grenades into passing troop trucks, some American soldiers easily came to see all Vietnamese as potential enemies, which made it all the more easy to take out this frustration and anxiety on any nearby civilians. The historian Christian Appy called this reliance on body counts, free-fire zones, and attrition a "doctrine of atrocity." These tactics encouraged a "patent disregard for human life" and all but institutionalized the mere gook rule, which dehumanized Vietnamese to the point of complete indifference. Said one frustrated American soldier, "You walk through the fucking bush for three days and nights without sleep. Watch your men, your buddies, your goddamn kids get booby-trapped. Blown apart. Get thrown six feet in the air by a trap laid by an old lady and come down with no legs." The solution, he straightforwardly concluded, "was to kill them all."[8]

Laws of War

To prevent American soldiers from "killing them all," the American military attempted to educate its personnel on proper conduct in combat. Since the early twentieth century, the various Hague and Geneva Conventions, with good intention, tried to define appropriate conduct and outlaw atrocious acts during war. The US Congress later codified similar definitions in the Uniform Code of Military Justice (UCMJ) and the Army further outlined these in its field manual titled *The Law of Land Warfare.* To commit a war crime, one must commit an atrocious act, such as murder, rape, assault, or mutilation, against *enemy* combatants or *enemy* noncombatants. *The Law of Land Warfare* stipulates that "war crimes are within the jurisdiction of general courts-martial" and that "violations of the law of war committed by persons subject to the military law of the United States will usually constitute violations of the Uniform Code of Military Justice, and, if so, will be prosecuted under that Code." Thus, an American soldier is not prosecuted for a "war crime" but rather for murder or rape or whatever article the soldier allegedly violated. In the case of My Lai, the Army charged those suspected in the killings with murder or assault with the intent to commit murder, or for related offenses, but not with war crimes per se.[9]

The UCMJ, its companion *Manual for Courts-Martial,* and *The Law of Land Warfare* also include valid defenses against charges commonly associated with war crimes. These defenses emerged from war crimes tribunals following World War II, which established the legal presumption that following orders did not excuse committing an atrocity (known as the Nuremberg Defense) and that commanders must be held responsible for acts committed by those under their command (known as the Yamashita Standard). In the UCMJ, for example, Article 90 allows for disobeying an unlawful order, but the burden of showing the order is unlawful is on the subordinate. Disobeying a lawful order forces the subordinate to determine the legality of an order, as described in Article 92: an order is unlawful if it is "contrary to the Constitution, the laws of the United States, or lawful superior orders" or "is beyond the authority of the official issuing it."[10] The *Manual for Courts-Martial* excuses an offense resulting from an unlawful order if the person who committed that offense believed the order to be lawful.[11] *The Law of Land Warfare* goes further:

> The fact that the law of war has been violated pursuant to an order of a superior authority, whether military or civil, does not deprive the act in question of its character of a war crime, nor does it constitute a defense in the trial of an accused individual, unless he did not know and could not reasonably have been expected to know that the act ordered was unlawful. In all cases where the order is held not to constitute a defense to an allegation of war crime, the fact that the individual was acting pursuant to orders may be considered in mitigation of punishment.[12]

All of this assumed, of course, that a nineteen-year-old private could recognize an unlawful order under combat conditions.

During basic training, inductees received minimal instruction on behavior in combat, forcing drill instructors to juxtapose teaching the laws of war with training young men to kill. In accordance with Army Regulation 350-216, this brief lesson outlined fundamental precepts, such as obligations of individual soldiers, rights of combatants and noncombatants, and the overall expectation of behavior during war. Regulation 350-216 also stipulated mandatory refresher training on the laws of war for every soldier once every twelve months, which theoretically meant that all soldiers in Vietnam received training in the laws of war during their twelve-month tour of duty. MACV also mandated additional training and issued numerous directives to educate soldiers on behavior toward combatants and noncombatants.[13]

In addition to a small pamphlet on how to operate and clean the M-16 rifle, a small phrase book, and a booklet called "Mines and Booby Traps," orientation packets for soldiers arriving in Vietnam included small reference cards to be carried at all times. One card contained the Army Code of Conduct, listing six points to guide soldiers' behavior, the last of which reminded a soldier to "never forget that I am an American fighting man, responsible for my actions, and dedicated to the principles which made my country free."[14] The orientation packet also included a card titled "The Enemy in Your Hands," designed to ensure proper treatment of captured enemy combatants. The card reminded soldiers that they "Cannot and Must Not: Mistreat a prisoner; Humiliate or degrade him; Take any of his personal effects which do not have significant military value; Refuse him medical treatment if required and available." One side of the card repeated to soldiers that "MISTREATMENT

OF ANY CAPTIVE IS A CRIMINAL OFFENSE. EVERY SOLDIER IS PERSONALLY RESPONSIBLE FOR THE ENEMY IN HIS HANDS," and detained personnel must "BE PROTECTED AGAINST VIOLENCE, INSULTS, CURIOSITY, AND REPRISALS OF ANY KIND."[15] Another card gave the "Nine Rules for Personnel of U.S. Military Assistance Command, Vietnam":

1. Remember we are guests here: We make no demands and seek no special treatment.
2. Join with the people! Understand their lives, use phrases from their language and honor their customs and laws.
3. Treat women with politeness and respect.
4. Make personal friends among the soldiers and common people.
5. Always give the Vietnamese the right of way.
6. Be alert to security and be ready to react with military skill.
7. Don't attract attention by loud, rude, or unusual behavior.
8. Avoid separating yourself from the people by a display of wealth or privilege.
9. Above all you are members of the U.S. Armed Forces on a difficult mission, responsible for all your official and personal actions. Reflect honor upon yourself and the United States of America.

The other side of the card warned soldiers that the Viet Cong would attempt to "turn the Vietnamese people against you," however, "You can defeat them at every turn by the strength, generosity, and understanding you display with the people."[16]

Officers arriving in Vietnam received a similar packet, with the added advice from a wallet-sized card titled "Guidance for Commanders in Vietnam." In addition to several guiding principles in dealing with the enemy militarily, the card advised field officers to use "firepower with care and discrimination, particularly in populated areas" and to keep troops "well informed, aware of the nine rules."[17]

Officers and enlisted personnel also received several directives on handling noncombatants. MACV Directive 525-3 offered guidance for "minimizing noncombatant casualties" during combat operations, warning that the enemy would "exploit fully incidents of noncombatant casualties and destruction of property" to "embitter the population, drive them into the arms of the VC, and make the long range goal of pacification more difficult and more costly." The directive discouraged preparatory fire in populated areas, concluding that any tactical gain would be "counterproductive in the long run" due to the risk of civilian casualties. According to the directive, commanders must instill in their troops the importance of "minimizing noncombatant casualties" through preoperation briefings to troops on rules of engagement and the location of civilians. Although American forces must be able to show the enemy that they could "move at will" and "defeat a VC force encountered," American troops must be mindful to "demonstrate constantly their concern for the safety of noncombatants."[18]

Other MACV directives provided guidelines for dealing with combatants and noncombatants as well as private property in combat situations. Directive 525-9 outlined procedures for dealing with private property, food supplies, and other material captured during combat operations and prohibited the destruction of dwellings and killing livestock unless warranted by the combat situation.[19] Several directives such as 381-46 and 190-3 outlined procedures for detaining and processing suspected Viet Cong and prisoners of war.[20]

MACV also issued guidelines for reporting and investigating war crimes and other crimes against noncombatants. MACV Directive 20-4, for example, clearly stated that "it is the responsibility of all military personnel having knowledge or receiving a report of an incident or of an act thought to be a war crime to make such incident known to his commanding officer as soon as practicable." The directive provided for the appointment of an investigating officer, submission of a formal report, including a copy to MACV, and maintenance of investigation records. MACV Directive 27-5 restated 20-4 with the intent to "reaffirm the prohibition against commission of war crimes and related acts."[21] US Army, Vietnam (USARV) Regulation 335-6 and MACV Directive 335-1 outlined reporting serious crimes or incidents, including such acts against Vietnamese civilians or property.[22] Further, Army Regulation 15-6 established procedures for inquiring into both war crimes and serious incidents.[23] Thus, prior to March 16, 1968, MACV had an established paper trail of policies, procedures, and directives to guide proper conduct and define, report, and investigate war crimes. Policies, procedures, and directives, however, served their purpose only as far as commanders enforced them and soldiers obeyed them.[24]

Charlie Company

Charlie Company belonged to the 1st Battalion, 20th Infantry, of the 11th Brigade, which had been assigned to the Americal Division in Vietnam. The Army established the original Americal Division in May 1942 by patching together units on New Caledonia, deriving *Americal* from the contraction of *American* and *Caledonia*. The Division served on Guadalcanal and in the Philippines during the Pacific war, then, after a brief stint on occupation duty in Japan, was deactivated in December 1945. The Americal returned briefly to serve in the Panama Canal Zone in 1954–1956 as the 23rd Infantry Division, then was reestablished in September 1967 for duty in Vietnam.[25]

The Americal Division replaced Task Force Oregon, which General Westmoreland established to conduct interdiction operations along the DMZ between North and South Vietnam. Like its World War II predecessor, the new Americal Division was patched together from other units. These units included the 196th Infantry Brigade, which had been in Vietnam since August 1966 and had been part of Task Force Oregon, and the 198th and 11th Infantry Brigades, both of which at this point remained in training in Texas and Hawaii, respectively. Because of its assigned area of operations, the Americal Division had operational control of several other units, including the 3rd Brigade of the 4th Infantry Division and the 1st Brigade of the 101st Airborne Division (which had also been part of Task Force Oregon), and the 3rd Brigade of the 1st Air Cavalry Division. By March 1968, the Americal consisted of the 196th, 198th, and 11th as the Division Brigades, plus various support units.

The 196th, 198th, and 11th Brigades had evolved into independent brigades and organized so that each supposedly could be quickly detached and reassigned to other commands with minimal disruption of existing Division command structures. Their creation also reflected strategic personnel needs, in particular the decision by the Johnson administration to rely upon the draft rather than calling up reserves to meet force requirements in the escalating war in Vietnam. Up to the Americal's reorganization into the 23rd Infantry Division in February 1969, none of these brigades could claim to be organic to the Division command structure, a situation that presented both personnel and operational challenges. Each brigade, for example, had standard operating procedures and other regulations unique to the unit. Considering that the brigades arrived in Vietnam at different times under unique conditions and in varying degrees of readiness, bringing them together under a single Division-wide set of procedures and regulations proved a laborious and ongoing task.[26]

In addition to the organizational abnormalities of the Americal, the twelve-month rotation policy caused significant problems common to all units in Vietnam. Enlisted personnel, noncommissioned officers, and officers constantly rotated in and out of the 198th and 11th Brigades as they completed their tours in Vietnam or arrived fresh from the United States. In order to adhere to unit strength requirements and maintain mandated ratios of new troops coming in to veterans rotating out, the Americal Division had to transfer troops between brigades in a sort of shell game. This so-called infusion program disrupted existing unit cohesion and structure, forcing troops to learn new procedures and become familiar with new commanders just when they had achieved such familiarity in their previous units.

Like all units in Vietnam, the Americal Division required lectures on the Code of Conduct, Geneva and Hague Conventions, the UCMJ and MACV directives on treatment of POWs (prisoners of war) as part of its regular training curriculum, as well as the annual two-hour refresher courses covering these issues for all personnel. The Americal Division also had procedures in place to investigate any allied or noncombatant casualties caused by artillery or errant airstrikes. Such procedures and training on paper placed the Americal in line with USARV, MACV, and Army regulations.[27]

Much of the direct command influence on Charlie Company came from its parent 11th Infantry Brigade. Stationed in Hawaii at Schofield Barracks, the 11th Infantry Brigade consisted of three infantry battalions when it received orders in the fall of 1967 to join the new Americal Division in Vietnam. Throughout February and March 1967, the 11th Infantry Brigade conducted company-level tactical exercises as part of its normal training regimen. Beginning in April, companies rotated through the Jungle Warfare Training Center in Hawaii, spending a week in intensive company- and platoon-level instruction that included exercises in securing a village and dealing with noncombatants.[28]

With personnel rotating in and out of the Brigade, reaching deployable status proved difficult, resulting in over 1,300 of its troops failing to meet criteria for approval to deploy to Vietnam. Over 400 infantrymen, already trained but new to the Brigade, joined the unit in Hawaii to help overcome this shortage while replacements continued to join the Brigade each week, which naturally wreaked havoc on unit training schedules. These pressures reduced eight-week training sequences to a mere four weeks, which resulted in "considerable confusion and caused significant turmoil in the brigade's personnel status which was detrimental to their pre-deployment preparation." As it deployed to Vietnam, the 11th Infantry Brigade remained several hundred troops under strength.

Once in Vietnam, the 11th Infantry Brigade was ordered to undergo additional training to make up for its abbreviated training schedule in Hawaii. Despite MACV's good intentions, however, orientation and operational training in country also suffered, cutting, for example, a week-long orientation course to just three days. The Brigade's companies dedicated time to helicopter combat assault training and ambush tactics during its first month in Vietnam, but even as the Brigade prepared for its first combat patrols, new personnel joined the unit, further aggravating the training experience for the entire Brigade. As disruptive as this appears, however, many units experienced similar problems in deploying to Vietnam.

Brigadier General Andrew Lipscomb commanded the 11th Infantry Brigade through its training in Hawaii and deployment to Vietnam. Lipscomb considered Charlie Company one of the Brigade's best, so much so that when he created Task Force Barker in January 1967 he assigned Charlie Company to it. Lipscomb, however, would not command the Brigade during the My Lai operation. Instead, the day before Charlie Company entered My Lai, Colonel Oran K. Henderson took over as Brigade commander. Henderson had commanded the Brigade briefly in 1966 and served as its executive officer. He had never commanded in combat.[29]

While other units participated in the March 16, 1968, operation in the Son My area, Charlie Company became the most infamous. In many ways, nothing unique or abnormal stood out about Charlie Company's personnel, training record, or combat performance up to March 16. As with many other units, predeployment training poorly prepared Charlie Company for the rigors of combat in Vietnam. Once there, the Company learned to fight through OJT, or "on the job training."

As a typical infantry company of three rifle platoons, a weapons platoon, and a headquarters platoon, Charlie Company had an authorized strength of 6 officers and 158 men when it deployed for Vietnam in December 1967. In March 1968, the Company had 5 officers to complement 125 troops. Draftees made up 61 percent of the enlisted personnel in the Company. Of these,

79 percent had graduated from high school. Fifty-three percent rated above normal on the Army's trainability scale and 59 percent scored above the standard in learning ability. In infantry aptitude, 46 percent scored above the norm. Enlistees or volunteers made up the remaining enlisted personnel in the Company. Fifty-six percent of these had a high school diploma, but the majority scored below the norm on trainability and learning ability. Sixty-one percent of enlistees, nevertheless, ranked above the norm in infantry aptitude. Taking draftees and enlistees together, 47 percent placed above the norm in trainability, compared to 52 percent Army-wide; 54 percent scored above the norm in learning ability, compared to 60 percent Army-wide; and 50 percent surpassed the norm for infantry, matching the Army-wide standard. While 70 percent had a high school diploma, only 8 percent came from Project 100,000 (compared to 12 percent across the Army).[30]

The troops in Charlie Company had a median age of twenty-two years for draftees and just under twenty-one years for enlistees. They came from all over the United States and from varying backgrounds, representing a cross section of ethnic and geographic diversity typical of Army infantry companies. Charlie Company's twenty-three NCOs had a median of twenty-two years in age and as a whole placed above the norm in trainability, learning ability, and infantry aptitude. Eighty-seven percent of them had graduated from high school (compared to 69 percent Army-wide) and a quarter of them had attended college. Sixty-six percent of the NCOs had enlisted, compared to 40 percent across the Army. In all, Charlie Company's NCO corps in March 1968 surpassed the Army norm.[31]

The commander of Charlie Company would play a central role in the coming events. Ernest L. Medina, a thirty-two-year-old captain of Mexican American descent from Springer, New Mexico, had been a company commander since 1966. Medina joined the Army from the National Guard as an enlisted man in 1956, serving in Germany and at Fort Riley, Kansas, before entering OCS at Fort Benning in 1964. Commissioned in March of that year, Medina stayed on at Fort Benning as a weapons instructor until 1966, when the Army sent him to Schofield Barracks, Hawaii, to be a company commander in the 11th Infantry Brigade. Medina made up for his lack of college education through energetic determination and able leadership, earning consistent exceptional/outstanding ratings. Under Medina's leadership, by December 1967 Charlie Company had acquired a reputation among many at Schofield Barracks as the best outfit in the 11th Brigade, earning Medina the respect of both superiors and subordinates, including that of Lieutenant William Calley. Medina's demanding training regimen and tough demeanor won him the nickname "Mad Dog Medina."[32]

William L. Calley, Jr., commanded Charlie Company's 1st Platoon at My Lai and would become the most controversial and enduring figure in the My Lai incident. Calley personified the popular cultural stereotype of the incompetent lieutenant in Vietnam. Born in Miami, Florida, in 1943, "Rusty" Calley had a normal early childhood, growing up in a middle-class home. In junior high, however, his grades suffered and he had to repeat the seventh grade for cheating on an exam. His parents sent him to the Georgia Military Academy, where under strict discipline he thrived through the tenth grade. He returned to public high school for his junior and senior year, where his grades again suffered, graduating in the lower quarter of his class of over seven hundred. Without prospects or real personal motivation, Calley enrolled at Palm Beach Junior College in 1963 but soon dropped out. After working several seasonal jobs, he landed a good position during a rail workers' strike with the Florida East Coast Railroad, but his job performance suffered from laziness and apathy. When striking workers returned to the job, Calley, without any seniority, took whatever menial tasks the railroad gave him. He quit in frustration in late 1965.

From there Calley bounced from job to job, while his family situation deteriorated (his mother had terminal cancer, dying in 1966, and his father's business went bankrupt). Working in Arizona in 1966, Calley made his way home to meet with his draft board in Miami after missing at least two draft notices. On the road and out of money in New Mexico, Calley contacted a local Army recruiting station in Albuquerque, where recruiters told him he could avoid the Miami draft board hassle by enlisting in New Mexico.

Even though the Army had rejected Calley in 1964 because of a failed physical, it now eagerly accepted him. Calley did his basic training at Fort Bliss, Texas, then completed the Adjutant General's Corps course at Fort Lewis, which qualified him as an Army clerk, a job in which he excelled. Legal historian Michal Belknap has speculated that, had Calley remained a clerk he probably would never have seen combat in Vietnam. By chance, however, a superior spotted Calley's attendance at the Georgia Military Academy on his record and sent Calley to OCS at Fort Benning, where he graduated 120th out of 156 in his training company. One can argue over whether a peacetime Army would have commissioned Calley, but the escalation of the war in Vietnam increased the demand for junior officers, so by form or function, Calley made it through OCS. The Army sent Calley to Schofield Barracks, where in the fall of 1967 he took command of 2nd Platoon in Medina's Charlie Company.[33]

Like other units at Schofield Barracks, Charlie Company had been both a pick-up point for new soldiers heading to Vietnam and a drop-off unit for veterans completing their tour to return to the United States. New personnel came and went, making Medina's efforts to establish regular training and unit cohesion extremely difficult. The changeover rate hit as high as 70 percent before Charlie Company left for Vietnam in December 1967, forcing Medina to use SP4s in positions normally held by seasoned sergeants (specialist 4th class was an enlisted rank, an E-4). Nevertheless, Mad Dog Medina pushed his company with firmness and resolve, as the unit successfully completed the Army Training Test and prepared to deploy to Vietnam. Before the unit left Hawaii, Lieutenant William Calley led a class session for Charlie Company called "Vietnam Our Host," in which he briefly covered cultural relations with the Vietnamese. Calley recalled his talk lasted only a few minutes, during which he listed several "dos and don'ts" while trying to keep the troops awake: "Oh God what a farce it was . . . I did a very very poor job of it," he later recalled.[34]

Medina, Calley, and Charlie Company arrived in Da Nang in early December 1967 aboard a Pan American Airways jet. From there, helicopters airlifted the unit to Landing Zone (LZ) Bronco in Quang Ngai Province, where the Company received three days of orientation that included limited combat assault training. Using a deserted village near Duc Pho as a training site, soldiers from the 2nd ARVN Division spent a day showing Charlie Company how to assault and secure a village and how to spot booby traps and mines. At LZ Carrington, located in a less active sector of Quang Ngai Province, Charlie Company conducted short-range patrols, making little contact with the enemy and spending much of its time screening Vietnamese in the numerous small villages and hamlets in the area. Charlie Company's first month in the war proved a quiet one.

Charlie Company's grace period ended in late January 1968, when it joined Task Force Barker. Named for its commander, Lieutenant Colonel Frank Barker, the Task Force consisted of several units cobbled together from various units of the Americal Division, numbering over 500 troops. Task Force Barker's area of operations (AO) included the Son Tinh District northeast of

Quang Ngai City. Unlike the comparatively pacified districts in which Charlie Company had operated in southern Quang Ngai Province, the northern region, particularly along the coast, remained under Viet Cong control. Task Force Barker took on the mission, codenamed Muscatine, to locate and destroy the Viet Cong 48th Local Force Battalion, which used this sector of Quang Ngai Province as a safe haven.[35]

Charlie Company now moved northeast of Quang Ngai City to LZ Dottie. Heavily defended by well-built bunkers, LZ Dottie sat like a fortified island in the middle of a Viet Cong–controlled sea of countryside. Charlie Company stood watch and patrolled near the base, and in short order suffered its first casualties, mostly from booby traps and mines. At LZ Dottie, Charlie Company could clearly hear the sounds and at night see the sights of the intense battle for nearby Quang Ngai City during the Tet Offensive. Yet at LZ Dottie, the attack passed in comparative quiet. As journalist Richard Hammer noted, Charlie Company's Tet experience resembled being in the "eye of a hurricane."[36]

The quiet, however, did not last. Soon after the battle for Quang Ngai subsided, Viet Cong units fled toward the comparative safety of the coastal hamlets, including the village complex of Son My. A productive agricultural region, it was a landscape dotted with lush green islands of bamboo trees and banana groves and dominated by rice paddies and irrigation canals. Local peasants built their homes near narrow trails and the few minor roads in these densely vegetated areas. Names on American maps rarely matched the names local villagers knew as their home. Son My had four administrative districts, or hamlets: Tu Cung, My Lai, My Khe, and Co Luy. The dozen or so villages within Son My had Vietnamese names, but American mapmakers had named each settlement according to the administrative district followed by a number. My Khe village (not My Khe administrative district) became My Lai (1) to the Americans, who commonly called the village "Pinkville" because of its color designation on maps. My Hoi village to the Vietnamese became My Khe (4) to the Americans. What the Americans called My Lai (4) local Vietnamese knew as Xom Lang and Binh Tay. American military intelligence seemed certain that the Viet Cong 48th Local Force Battalion used several of the hamlets as safe havens and staging areas and My Lai (1) as the Battalion's headquarters.[37]

Task Force Barker hoped to trap and destroy the 48th Local Force Battalion, but Charlie Company patrolled in a fruitless search for the Viet Cong

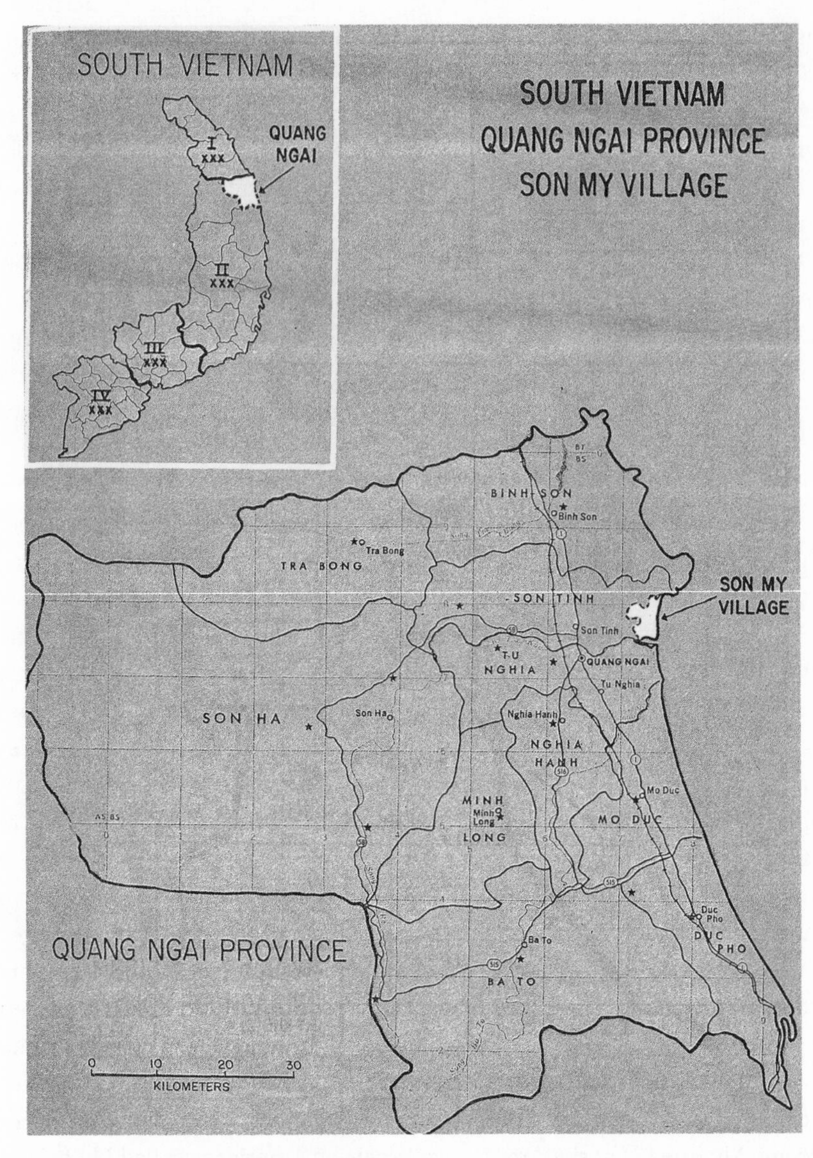

Orientation map of South Vietnam, Quang Ngai Province, and Son My village, used in the Peers Inquiry. Peers Inquiry, Vol. 1, Bk. 1, Sketch 3-1.

unit, finding instead only booby traps and the occasional sniper. The monotonous patrolling did not come without cost, however, as the Company lost a soldier here and another there. On February 12, Calley led his platoon back into an area where the previous day the Company had encountered Viet Cong small-arms fire. Again encountering sniper fire, Calley rerouted the platoon, inexplicably allowing his troops to walk exposed along the top of an earthen dike. A sniper's bullet hit SP4 William Weber, Calley's radio telephone operator (RTO), tearing "his kidney out" and killing him within minutes. Charlie Company had suffered its first fatality, all because Calley, as he later admitted, had behaved like a "fool" by needlessly exposing his men to the sniper. Later that night at LZ Uptight, Task Force Barker's other firebase, Calley gave a patently false body count, reporting his platoon had killed six Viet Cong in an attempt to justify the loss of Weber.[38]

Task Force Barker had its first big fight on February 13 while attempting to trap the 48th Local Force Battalion north of Son My. In a three-day operation, involving Alpha, Bravo, and Charlie Companies, the Task Force claimed eighty Viet Cong killed to the loss of three American dead and fifteen wounded but no weapons captured. The next substantial action took place on February 23, as Alpha and Bravo Companies again tried to snare the 48th Local Force Battalion. In two days, they killed seventy-eight Viet Cong while losing only three killed and twenty-eight wounded. The 48th, however, remained intact and at large.

Charlie Company suffered its worst loss on February 25. While on patrol, several troops walked into a minefield. Explosions hurled men and shattered equipment, causing others to panic and set off more mines. Medina stayed cool amidst the bedlam, working quickly and fearlessly to get his men out of harm's way. With a medic, he brought aid to the wounded while directing men with mine detectors to clear a path out of the area. The explosions killed three men and wounded at least sixteen others. A booby trap killed another man after the minefield incident. Medina vividly recalled the sight of one of the dead: "He was split as if somebody had taken a cleaver and right from his crotch all the way up to his chest cavity." The Army rewarded Medina's courage with a Silver Star, its third highest decoration for valor. Having just enjoyed a three-day pass, Calley returned to LZ Dottie just as the medevacs (medical evacuation helicopters) arrived with the wounded from the minefield. Calley clearly recalled helping unload one of the helicopters and seeing pairs of bloody combat boots, some with feet still in them. When

Charlie Company returned later that day, Calley thought they had changed: "It seemed like a different company now."[39]

Weeks of frustration at fighting an enemy they rarely saw approached a crisis point. Mines and booby traps caused most of Charlie Company's casualties. The strain showed. Several men began treating Vietnamese, even children, harshly, whereas before they had been more generous toward local villagers. Many in the Company believed the Vietnamese intentionally did not warn them about the minefield. Lieutenant Roger Alaux, the Company's forward artillery observer, later recalled "these people are just as much VC as the ones that actually planted those minefields."[40] On March 14, the Company lost another man, Sergeant George Cox, to a mine. At a memorial service for Cox on March 15, Medina told Charlie Company that the next day they would have a chance to get revenge for Cox and their other lost comrades.

2 March 16, 1968

That evening, as we cleaned our weapons and got our gear ready, we talked about the operation. People were talking about killing everything that moved. Everyone knew what we were going to do.

PFC Robert Pendleton, Charlie Company

What happened in Son My on March 16, 1968, is difficult to describe. The sheer brutality of the atrocities staggers the imagination. Reconstructing the actions of the soldiers of Task Force Barker in Son My is also fraught with difficulties. The soldiers and civilians at Son My tell a similar story, but the details can vary, in some cases widely. Thousands of pages of testimony collected by the Army's investigations, congressional hearings, and the trials produce a general picture of the events of that day. Although dozens of American soldiers participated in the March 16 operation, each person nonetheless had a unique experience. No individual saw the totality of what happened. Investigators interviewed witnesses months, and in some cases years, after the event occurred. For those still in uniform, fear of prosecution may have influenced testimony, just as freedom from prosecution for those already honorably discharged may have influenced what they told investigators. Despite these difficulties, the basic events of that day can generally be reconstructed, but a complete, definitive picture will likely never be known.[1]

March 15, 1968

Lieutenant Colonel Frank Barker issued verbal orders for the Son My operation on the afternoon of March 15, 1968. Barker did not write out a formal operational order; rather, his officers stood in a loose circle outside his command bunker at LZ Dottie and listened while Barker outlined the coming operation. Barker's plan for the Son My area on the next day appeared straightforward, not unlike hundreds of similar operations American forces conducted throughout the Vietnam War.

Captain Eugene Kotouc's intelligence briefing confirmed what the officers of Task Force Barker expected. The Viet Cong 48th Local Force Battalion controlled the area, using either My Lai (4) or My Lai (1) as a headquarters or staging area. As Task Force Barker's S-2 (intelligence officer), Kotouc told them that villagers would likely be on their way to market by the time Bravo and Charlie Companies reached their landing zones. Viet Cong and Viet Cong sympathizers inhabited the entire area, so Kotouc warned them to expect "heavy resistance." Based upon their previous experience in Son My, Captain Medina and other officers expected a tough fight.

The operational plan called for a brief artillery barrage near the landing zones, then helicopters would deliver Task Force Barker's troops to their target sites. Charlie Company's 1st and 2nd Platoons would sweep through My Lai (4) from west to east followed by 3rd Platoon to destroy bunkers, buildings, and food caches. As Charlie Company made its way through My Lai (4), platoons from Bravo Company, 4th Battalion, 3rd Infantry, would approach My Lai (1) from the south to north, heading just west of what American maps called My Khe (4) along the coast. Bravo Company and Charlie Company would then converge on My Lai (1) to flush the Viet Cong of the 48th Local Force Battalion toward the north, where Alpha Company, 3rd Battalion, 1st Infantry, lay in wait, acting as the anvil for Bravo and Charlie Companies' hammer. Swift boats from the US Navy would patrol the coast to the east to encourage Viet Cong flight northward toward Alpha Company. An aero-scout team consisting of one OH-23 "Bubble" light observation helicopter and two UH-1B gunships from Bravo Company, 123rd Aviation Battalion, would act as a screen to block any enemy attempting to withdraw to the south along Route 521.[2]

Colonel Oran K. Henderson, who had just taken command of the 11th Infantry Brigade, also addressed the officers of Task Force Barker, encourag-

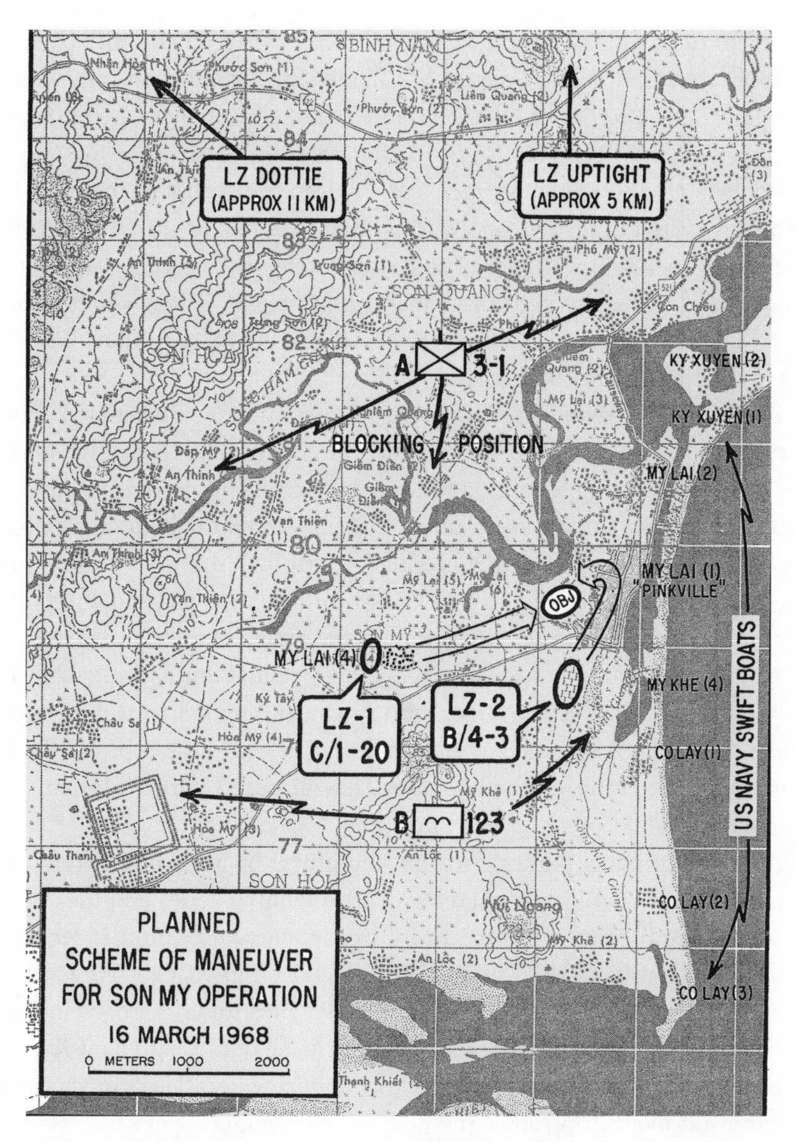

Map of Charlie Company's planned scheme of maneuver, as determined from testimony gathered by the Peers Inquiry. Peers Inquiry, Vol. 1, Bk. 1, Sketch 5-2.

ing them to move swiftly and make sure they confirmed kills and collected weapons and equipment. Captain Medina recalled Henderson's attention to this point: "He emphasized that he wanted the troops to be aware of this and that they should be aggressive in closing with and destroying the enemy." Henderson also noted that women and children could not only help the Viet Cong get away but also escape with weapons, as had occurred in previous operations in which units failed to capture weapons and other equipment. Henderson finished his pep talk by telling his officers, "When we get through with that 48th Battalion, they won't be giving us anymore trouble. We're going to do them in once and for all."

Both Captain Medina and Captain Kotouc later testified that Lieutenant Colonel Barker ordered the destruction of livestock, foodstuffs, homes, and other structures. According to Kotouc, Barker said he "wanted the area cleaned out, he wanted it neutralized, and he wanted the buildings knocked down." Since they assumed Viet Cong controlled the area, determining whether property belonged to Viet Cong or innocent civilians did not occur to anyone. Likewise, Barker issued no specific orders as to detaining and processing noncombatants. As a search and destroy mission with the objective of wiping out a Viet Cong force, its very nature implied total destruction. While no one later alleged Barker specifically ordered his troops to kill civilians encountered during the operation, few disputed Barker's intention to eliminate all Viet Cong and Viet Cong sympathizers.

After the briefing, Barker, Medina, and others boarded helicopters to fly over the area to familiarize themselves with landing zones and the general lay of the land. After returning to LZ Dottie, company commanders went back to their units to brief their platoon leaders and NCOs. "We have had a lot of trouble down there," Captain Earl Michles told his troops in Bravo Company. The time had come to "clean the place out." Lieutenant Kenneth Boatman, the forward observer for Bravo Company, recalled "everybody was enthusiastic about going down there . . . We were going to get rid of it—clean the place out."

At an emotional memorial service for Sergeant Cox, Medina spoke of the men Charlie Company had lost, leaving a "definite impression" that the operation would be the Company's best opportunity to get revenge for their dead and wounded comrades. He then gathered his officers and with a shovel drew in the dirt the operational movements of the morning's mission. Medina told them that the Viet Cong would outnumber them as much as two to one and that Charlie Company should expect "heavy contact," perhaps the "heaviest contact we had ever been in." Several anticipated that they "were going to search and probably burn a lot." Lieutenant Calley claimed Medina had said that any people remaining in My Lai (4) would be Viet Cong: "All civilians had left the area, there were no civilians in the area. And anyone there would be considered enemies."[3]

Throughout the night, soldiers prepared for the early morning operation. They cleaned weapons and packed food, water, ammunition, medical supplies, and other gear while talking about what awaited them in the morning. Private Dennis Conti, of 1st Platoon, Charlie Company, anticipated fierce Viet Cong resistance, describing his comrades as "really psyched up" and "ready to meet a foe of equal military strength, if not greater." Sergeant Isaiah Cowan, also of Charlie Company's 1st Platoon, remembered Captain Medina telling them that "everything that was in the village would be Viet Cong or Viet Cong suspects." Cowan believed Charlie Company had a tough day of fighting ahead: "We were under the impression that we would be hit by a large volume of fire coming from the VC." Sergeant John Smail, a squad leader in 1st Platoon, believed "We were really going in to get hit by a really big force. We carried extra ammo, as we did on other occasions, but this one seemed more intense. We were really going to make good contact." SP4 Fernando Trevino, of Charlie Company's 2nd Platoon, assumed Son My would be dangerous: "We knew that Pinkville was a pretty bad area for booby traps and that we had been shot at quite a few times before. We had been around that place, so we knew it was a pretty bad area into which we were going."

Others noted a desire for retribution, a chance to get "revenge for some of our fallen comrades." Sergeant Michael Bernhardt, of Charlie Company's 2nd Platoon, sensed the Company was "going to wreak some vengeance on someone." Private Tommy Moss, also of 2nd Platoon, recalled that "it seemed like it was a chance to get revenge or something like that for the lives we had lost." SP4 Gregory Olsen, a member of 2nd Platoon's machine gun squad, remembered Medina telling them that they could now "even the score with Charlie" (slang for Viet Cong; derived from military phonetic alphabet for the initials VC, or Victor Charlie). The talk of revenge echoed among the men that night, recalled SP4 Thomas Kinch: "That's the way I took it, to my knowledge, that they wanted revenge on the village, for what had happened." Sergeant David Hein, of Charlie Company's mortar platoon, wanted to "get in there and get these people that shot our men." Sergeant Joe Jolly vividly remembered, "We were loaded for bear . . . people were more or less out for vengeance."

Captain Medina recalled his own anxiety about the operation: "We would probably take heavy casualties . . . I was quite concerned about it." Lieutenant Calley later wrote of his own fears, "I was afraid . . . Everyone was." Calley claimed he offered a prayer before the mission: "Help us be good soldiers tomorrow. Help us make the right decisions: amen."[4]

March 16, 1968—Morning

It sounds trite to suggest that for Task Force Barker the operation in the early morning hours of March 16, 1968, began like any other. The discordant clatter of equipment, troops rechecking their weapons, the sharp shouts of commands, and the choking dust kicked up by helicopter rotors as troops prepared to board their transports would have been familiar. The uneasy tension common before a combat operation, too, would have been present. The scene probably looked like the initial moments of hundreds of other air assault operations that American forces conducted across South Vietnam from 1965 through 1972.

Even with these familiar sights and sounds, the day had a distinctly, if not morosely, different feel. The previous days had been difficult ones. Sergeant Cox's memorial service had upset many in Charlie Company. The pep talks had made their mark. The multiday operation about to kick off that morning gave every indication of being intense. The men expected a tough fight. They knew the dangers of Quang Ngai Province and knew that some of their comrades would not survive it.

From the 174th Assault Helicopter Company, five UH-1 lift helicopters—commonly known as "Hueys" or "slicks" but called "Dolphins" by the crews of the 174th, for their radio call signs—and two UH-1 gunships, called "Sharks," touched down at LZ Dottie just after 0700 hours to begin the lift to My Lai (4). Four additional UH-1 gunships from the 71st Assault Helicopter Company, nicknamed "Firebirds" for their radio call signs by the 71st, joined them at the LZ. Charlie Company's 1st and 2nd Platoons, along with Captain Medina's command group, boarded for the eleven-kilometer flight to Son My and the hamlet of My Lai (4). In the dust and debris kicked up by the roaring helicopters, troops burdened with as much as sixty pounds of ammunition and gear struggled to get seated in the tightly packed helicopters. Calley noted the adrenaline rush as the helicopters lifted off: "We felt as automobile racers do. A split second and I might hit the very edge of disaster."[5] They had packed heavy for this mission, carrying extra ammunition in the expectation of intense fighting over the next few days.

As the first wave took off from LZ Dottie at about 0715 hours, Lieutenant Colonel Barker's command and control helicopter, "Charlie 6," already patrolled the airspace in the vicinity of Son My. Barker radioed fire adjustment coordinates as artillery fire pounded the area around the target LZ and the extreme western edge of My Lai (4). From several kilometers away at LZ Uptight, four 105mm guns fired as many as 120 rounds in about five minutes, timed to end as the first assault wave arrived at the target LZ. As the Sharks and Dolphins approached from the south to avoid incoming artillery rounds, door gunners sprayed preparatory fire around the target LZ. Despite expectations and even initial radio reports that the LZ would be "hot," they encountered no enemy fire. While helicopter crews spotted some Viet Cong in the vicinity and actually killed some with gunfire, crews in the choppers circling immediately above the LZ saw no enemy, nor did they receive fire near the LZ.

At approximately 0730 hours, troops from Charlie Company jumped from their helicopters, hovering just a few feet above the ground. As soon as they cleared the doors, the Dolphins, now unburdened, quickly roared upward and headed back to LZ Dottie to collect 3rd Platoon. Now on the ground, squads spread out around the LZ, firing in all directions to secure the area in the expectation of heavy enemy resistance. No enemy, however, fired upon them. Declaring the LZ "cold," Captain Medina ordered both platoons to deploy their squads in defensive positions around the LZ to await the second wave. Within twenty minutes, 3rd Platoon joined 1st and 2nd Platoons on the ground. Charlie Company then cautiously moved eastward toward My Lai (4).

Meanwhile, throughout Son My villagers went about their morning routines, very much as preceding generations had done before them. They performed their chores, cooked meals, and went to work, as they always had. Some visited family in neighboring hamlets, while others came to My Lai (4) for the same purpose. The morning's activity, however, did not include large numbers of villagers making their way to market, nor did it include the 48th Viet Cong Local Force Battalion, which had moved out of the area and largely scattered during the previous few nights. Pham Thi Don, a fifty-one-year-old woman, later told investigators that although Viet Cong came into the villages almost every night, the few who had been in the area on the night of March 15 had mostly fled before the Americans arrived.[6]

The sudden eruption of artillery rounds obliterated this pastoral existence. Terrified families ran for their lives to nearby bunkers or trenches. Others fled, searching for cover behind embankments or in the surrounding rice paddies. Some remained in their homes, too frightened to move. Pham Lai and his family finished breakfast, then as he prepared to leave for work the sudden barrage sent them dashing to a trench near their home. Do Ba, a fifteen-year-old boy, was working alone at his family home when the shelling began. His parents had already left for work in a nearby village, while his five younger sisters had stayed the night with family friends in My Lai (4). He ran to a shelter next to the house. Le Tong and his family had just walked out of their home on their way to work when artillery shells began to fall. They quickly sought protection in a nearby bunker. Nguyen Thi Nhung had gone to work in the rice fields early on that Saturday morning. She saw artillery strike My Lai (4) and heard the helicopters approaching. For over an hour, she hid in the rice paddy with only her head barely above water. Hearing artillery fire and seeing approaching helicopters, fourteen-year-old Pham Thua hid in a bunker with his family.

Within half an hour after the shelling stopped, villagers could see American soldiers approaching their homes. Viet Cong units in the area had long since fled, while remaining individuals and small teams went to ground in hiding. For the men of Task Force Barker, expecting heavy fighting and no villagers, seeing so many peasants came as quite a surprise. Based upon prior experience in the area and what they had been told in their briefings, many soldiers naturally assumed anyone they encountered in these ostensibly peaceful hamlets would be Viet Cong, or at the very least Viet Cong sympathizers. These peasants therefore must be the enemy. The general rule of thumb held that Viet Cong ran away, while friendly villagers stayed put because they, supposedly, had nothing to fear. That morning, many villagers in and around My Lai (4) would have plenty to fear.

Initially, everything seemed to be going according to Barker's plan as Charlie Company advanced toward My Lai (4). Lieutenant Calley and 1st Platoon moved toward the southern end of the village, while Lieutenant Stephen Brooks and 2nd Platoon approached the hamlet's northern end. Third Platoon remained with Captain Medina's command group in reserve, forming a defensive line on the western edge of My Lai (4). After 1st and 2nd Platoons swept through the village, Charlie Company's operational plan had 3rd Platoon following close behind to burn houses, destroy bunkers, and process detained prisoners. They had yet to receive any enemy fire, nor had Charlie Company triggered any booby traps or mines.

As Charlie Company moved toward My Lai (4), Sharks south of the hamlet spotted, engaged, and killed at least four armed Viet Cong attempting to flee the area. Aircrews dropped smoke markers to alert squads on the ground of the locations of the bodies so they could collect weapons and other gear and confirm the kills. A few isolated Viet Cong did roam the area but not in force as expected. As they approached the village, both 1st and 2nd Platoons laid down heavy fire on any place that might hide Viet Cong. Any patch of thick vegetation or spot that looked like a bunker received bursts of preemptive fire. Men from both platoons fired upon the few peasants who showed themselves, killing several before reaching the hamlet. Fleeing Vietnamese trying to hide in the rice fields to the northwest of the hamlet also drew American fire.

Expecting sniper fire and booby traps, 1st and 2nd Platoons cautiously entered the hamlet just before 0800 hours. Calley placed Sergeant David Mitchell's 1st Squad to the right, or south, and Sergeant L. G. Bacon's 2nd Squad on the left, or north, of their approach. To the north of 1st Platoon, Lieutenant Brooks oriented 2nd Platoon's 1st Squad under Sergeant Kenneth Hodges on the left, Sergeant Kenneth Schiel's 2nd Squad in the center, and Sergeant Lawrence LaCroix's 3rd Squad to the right. As 1st Platoon began firing into the southwestern edge of My Lai (4), 2nd Platoon laid down thick fire on the northwestern part of the hamlet.

Flying above the operation in his command helicopter, Lieutenant Colonel Barker reported to the Tactical Operations Center (TOC) at LZ Dottie that all three platoons had landed and that 3rd Platoon's 3rd Squad had moved south to collect weapons from the Viet Cong killed by the Sharks. By the time Lieutenant Jeffrey LaCross and 3rd Platoon's 3rd Squad reached the area where the Viet Cong had been killed, the smoke marker had burned out. They searched the area and initially failed to find any weapons, but Captain Medina ordered them to continue the search. Medina's insistence paid off, as a short time later Private Michael Terry discovered an M-1 carbine. Operational success depended in part upon the number of weapons captured; now,

Ronald Haeberle's photograph of a burning structure at My Lai (4) on March 16, 1968, testifies to the true nature of a search and destroy mission. The soldier in the photograph is identified as SP5 Nicholas Capezza. Peers Inquiry, Vol. 3, Bk. 6, P-35, Haeberle color photograph #12A.

Charlie Company had captured one weapon. Barker also relayed Captain Medina's report that Charlie Company had already killed fifteen Viet Cong in just over half an hour, despite no enemy contact or fire received.[7]

Major Robert McKnight, the 11th Brigade S-3 (operations officer) flying with Colonel Henderson, radioed Barker that he could clearly see approximately three hundred people "moving out of the operational area in an orderly manner" along Route 521. Hundreds of villagers fled Son My, among them Viet Cong attempting to blend in with refugees. Sharks flying above soon spotted another Viet Cong, armed and carrying ammunition boxes, running along Route 521. As helicopters tracked the Viet Cong near the road, frightened refugees squatted nearby to avoid fire from the Sharks, which soon found their target.[8]

Private Jay Roberts, an Army correspondent, and Sergeant Ronald Haeberle, a Signal Corps photographer, had arrived with the second lift. Roberts, from Arlington, Virginia, accompanied the operation to write a story on the day's action for the brigade public information office. Haeberle, a native of Cleveland, Ohio, carried his Army camera, with which he took the familiar photographs that later appeared in *Stars and Stripes* and newspapers back in the United States. On black and white film, he captured troops advancing from the LZ and setting fire to hootches and other structures. The 11th Brigade Information Office had its photographers use black and white film because newspapers preferred it to color images. Haeberle also carried his personal camera, loaded with color film. He hoped to use his color slides as part of a lecture about his experience in the war for local civic clubs and other groups upon his return home to Ohio. In the field, Haeberle likened his performance with a camera to an infantryman with a rifle—reacting, aiming, shooting. The images he captured would become the most explosive pictures taken during the war.

Haeberle and Roberts followed 3rd Squad as it advanced toward Route 521, where they spotted the Vietnamese refugees heading southwest. In the air above, Shark crewmembers watched as soldiers of 3rd Squad fired into the group of approximately fifty Vietnamese, killing at least three but perhaps as many as fifteen. In his testimony to the Peers Inquiry, Lieutenant LaCross only mentioned "some firing" ahead of his position in the line, which had stretched to over one hundred meters. PFC Robert T'Souvas recalled the Squad firing at the Vietnamese; so, too, did SP4 Frank Beardslee. Haeberle and Roberts also testified that they both saw troops from 3rd Squad fire into the group of refugees at a distance of about seventy-five meters, killing at least three or four "military-aged males."

After crossing the road, 3rd Squad came upon a woman hiding in a ditch near a rice field. Helicopter crews saw a soldier shoot and kill the woman. Haeberle also saw the shooting, claiming that initially one soldier fired at her, then others "opened up on her." Haeberle later told investigators, "She was hit in the head and you could see a piece of her skull fly up in the air." After finding another weapon and the ammunition boxes, 3rd Squad turned around and headed back toward My Lai (4) to rejoin 3rd Platoon. Along the way, they allegedly killed two more Vietnamese running away from the hamlet and shot some livestock. Some in the Squad may also have shot down another small group of Vietnamese civilians before rejoining their unit.[9]

While 3rd Squad conducted its reconnaissance along Route 521 and the rest of 3rd Platoon set up its defensive perimeter west of My Lai (4), 1st and 2nd Platoons moved through the hamlet. Thick vegetation—banana trees, bamboo, elephant grass, hedgerows—made keeping formation difficult. One could not see more than several yards in any direction. Squads crossed lines, intermingling with each other. Operational control all but evaporated.

Soldiers from both platoons cleared homes and rounded up villagers. They shot livestock—cows, pigs, ducks, and water buffalo. Soldiers destroyed caches of rice and other foodstuffs with fragmentation grenades. Such tactics would have appeared normal for veterans of similar search and destroy operations, except that neither platoon received enemy fire. And, they began killing men, women, and children. Some raped and sodomized young girls, mothers, and elderly women, then killed them. A few purportedly mutilated corpses, cutting off ears and even heads. Things were going horribly wrong.

It would take some time that morning before anyone realized the scale of the killing as 1st and 2nd Platoons moved through My Lai (4). The limited line of sight and sounds of close-order gunfire convinced several soldiers that their comrades had engaged Viet Cong forces, putting everyone on edge. No one officer or NCO could actually see the whole situation. They expected sizable Viet Cong resistance and no innocent civilians in the area. They knew that any Vietnamese could be Viet Cong and should either be rounded up and brought rearward for interrogation or shot on sight if running away. Such a rational explanation, however, belies the fact that several soldiers became enmeshed in a killing frenzy that seemed to have no other purpose other than to satisfy an urge to kill.

2nd Platoon in My Lai (4) and Binh Tay

Lieutenant Brooks and 2nd Platoon entered the northwestern part of My Lai, having already killed several Vietnamese peasants. As they approached the hamlet, a woman came out of a hut crying and carrying a baby. Brooks allegedly ordered Private Varnado Simpson to shoot the woman. "Acting on his orders," Simpson later explained, "I shot the woman and her baby." PFC Dean Fields heard the order and saw Simpson shoot the woman from a distance of about twenty-five meters. Simpson claimed SP4 Floyd Wright, SP4 Max Hutson, and SP4 Charles Hutto then entered the hut and shot and killed several children who remained inside.[10]

The operation seemed to devolve into a fury of shooting and killing. Children approached the platoon expecting handouts of gum and chocolate, cheerfully shouting "chop, chop." Soldiers allegedly cut them down with semiautomatic fire from their M-16 assault rifles. Villagers emerged from bunkers and hiding places as the shelling subsided, only to be shot by approaching Americans. When no one came out of bunker holes and houses after repeated shouts of "lai day" (come here), soldiers tossed in grenades or simply sprayed the hovels with bullets, killing or wounding whomever remained inside. According to investigators, 2nd Platoon "neither sought to take nor did they retain any prisoners, suspects, or detainees" as they moved through My Lai (4) that morning.

Members of 2nd Platoon killed as if following some alternative standard operating procedure. Sergeant Kenneth Schiel, leader of 1st Squad, 2nd Platoon, forced several villagers out of their home then allegedly shot them. He supposedly said at the time, "I don't want to do it, but I have to do it because we were ordered to do it." Dean Fields, who served as Lieutenant Brooks's radio operator, later commented on the platoon's calm efficiency: "They were doing a good job, and they were doing it, more or less, because they were told . . . They were not out of control." "After they left one hootch, they went to another hootch expecting to find more they could kill," Fields recalled. "I know for a fact they didn't hate to do it."

In one instance, as several men stood guard over a group of men, women, and children, Private Gary Roschevitz allegedly boasted that he wanted to try out his M-79 grenade launcher, which he had apparently not yet had the opportunity to use in combat. Hutto, Private James M. McBreen, and several others witnessed Roschevitz back away several meters to stand on top of a small rise, then fire at least two, but perhaps as many as four, rounds into the middle of the group, killing several and wounding the rest. Other members of 2nd Platoon then killed the survivors with small arms.[11]

Roschevitz also purportedly stopped members of 1st Platoon as they took a small group of men, women, and children rearward for screening. He attempted to take Private Roy Wood's M-16 to shoot them, but Wood refused to give up his weapon. Hutto and Wood watched as Roschevitz then turned to Simpson, forcibly took his M-16 away, shot at least five Vietnamese, including a woman and two girls, then casually returned the weapon to Simpson. Roschevitz later bragged to Private Johnnie Tunstal about the killing.[12]

At about 0830 hours, Medina radioed Lieutenant Brooks to move his platoon north of My Lai (4) to collect weapons and gear of two Viet Cong killed by the Sharks. Smoke markers led the men of 2nd Platoon to the location, where they quickly found the two bodies along with two weapons. Instead of returning to My Lai (4), Medina ordered Brooks to move his platoon on to the nearby hamlet of Binh Tay, where according to the Peers Inquiry 2nd Platoon "continued the pattern of burning, killings, and rapes which it had followed inside My Lai (4)."

In Binh Tay, PFC Leonard Gonzales recalled seeing several rapes and killings. He tried to help a sixteen-year-old girl, whom he claimed had been assaulted by Sergeant Kenneth Hodges, by having her stick close to him in the hope that she would not be killed. "If left on her own," Gonzales believed, "someone would have killed her." Gonzales came upon a pile of bodies, all women and girls, and all naked. Roschevitz stood nearby with his grenade launcher. When Gonzales asked what had happened to the women, Roschevitz said he had forced them all to undress so that he could have sex with them, threatening to shoot all of them if they refused. They refused, apparently, and Roschevitz allegedly fired at least two M-79 buckshot rounds into the huddled group. Gonzales recalled staring in shock at their naked bodies, intact except for the tiny holes caused by the buckshot.[13]

Around 0930 hours, Captain Medina radioed Lieutenant Brooks to "cease fire" and "stop killing" in Binh Tay. Why Medina issued this order is unclear, as at the time Medina and his command group physically remained in My Lai (4) and could not have seen the killing taking place in Binh Tay. Medina further ordered Brooks and 2nd Platoon to burn the hootches, then round up the remaining villagers and move them out of Binh Tay. Brooks and 2nd Platoon gathered approximately sixty villagers and shepherded them toward the southwest away from the area to safety.

1st Platoon in My Lai (4)

The acts perpetrated by members of 1st Platoon later became synonymous with My Lai in American popular memory. Lieutenant Calley and several of his men entered My Lai (4) with guns blazing. They fired into hootches, tossed grenades into bunkers, and shot at the Vietnamese fleeing the hamlet. They gathered large groups of villagers, herded them into ditches, and shot them down. In a matter of hours, soldiers of 1st Platoon killed hundreds of men, women, and children.

Accounts of the killing illustrate the difficulty of explaining what happened that day. For example, while members of 1st Platoon rounded up villagers, presumably for screening, SP4 Allen Boyce captured a Vietnamese man, a farmer between forty and fifty years old. As he detained the man, Private Harry Stanley claimed, Boyce suddenly bayoneted the man in the chest then shot him dead. Boyce then "ran over to another Vietnamese person, an old man, and grabbed him and threw him in a well, and then threw a hand grenade down behind him." When asked who else witnessed Boyce throw the man down the well, Stanley replied, "Everybody that was in the squad, I guess. Mostly everybody anyway." Other members of the Squad, however, denied seeing either event take place.[14]

SP4 Robert Maples and PFC James Bergthold made up a machine gun team in Sergeant L. G. Bacon's squad in Charlie Company's 1st Platoon. Bergthold later recalled that despite receiving no enemy fire, "they [Charlie Company] were firing all over. Everybody was firing. I don't know why they were firing so much." He and Maples herded several people out of a hootch, where one man remained on the floor, shot through both legs. Bergthold took out his .45 pistol and at close range fired, blowing off the top of the man's head. Bergthold later claimed he killed the man "to put him out of his misery."[15]

Amid the killing, several men of 1st Platoon gathered villagers and brought them to Lieutenant Calley for screening. Privates Herbert Carter, Paul Meadlo, Dennis Conti, and James Dursi were holding a group of about fifty Vietnamese, including many women and children when Lieutenant Calley approached and ordered his soldiers to "take care of them." The soldiers assumed Calley simply meant for them to guard the detainees. Calley pressed on with his radio operator, SP4 Charles Sledge, following close behind.

Medina radioed Calley, demanding to know why his movement through My Lai (4) had not progressed more quickly. Calley replied that processing so many detained Vietnamese slowed down his platoon. Later, Calley claimed that Medina told him to get moving, to "get rid of 'em," to "waste all those goddamn people." Calley apparently took this to mean to kill the villagers. Medina later said he meant for Calley to get moving because of the uncertain situation—he expected to run into the Viet Cong 48th Local Force Battalion at any moment.[16]

A short while later, Calley and Sledge returned to Meadlo, Conti, Carter, Dursi, and others standing watch over the crowd of Vietnamese. Meadlo alleged that Calley excitedly demanded to know why he had not killed them. According to Meadlo and Conti, Calley told the men, "I want them killed" and ordered the men to shoot the gathered prisoners. Calley and Meadlo began firing into the men, women, and children with their M-16 rifles. Both men used several magazines. Meadlo stopped firing and began to cry. He apparently tried to pass his M-16 to Conti to finish the job with Calley, but Conti refused. Meadlo claimed that Stanley and Private Daniel Simone also joined in the melee but that Dursi did not fire into the ditch. Stanley and Simone denied participating in the killings. After firing into the ditch several more times, Calley grabbed Sledge and moved on.[17]

Calley then approached another large group of detained villagers near an irrigation ditch. Several soldiers claimed Meadlo, Boyce, and Sergeant Mitchell helped Calley push men, women, and children into the ditch. Simone, Sledge, Stanley, and others watched as Calley ordered Meadlo and Boyce to shoot them all. Private Ronald Grzesik questioned an old Buddhist monk nearby, who was so frightened and shocked at what had been happening around him he could hardly speak. Calley demanded to know the whereabouts of Viet Cong and the locations of weapons caches. Frustrated, Calley struck the old man in the mouth with the butt of his M-16. Stanley repeatedly questioned the monk in Vietnamese, but the monk only replied that the village contained no Viet Cong and no weapons. According to Sledge, Calley then threw the monk into a rice paddy and shot him in the head at close range. Calley later admitted hitting the monk but denied shooting him. While they questioned the man, a two-year-old boy tried to crawl out of the ditch of dead and wounded. Sledge and Stanley witnessed Calley throw the boy back into the ditch and shoot him.[18]

The killing went on for another hour. More detained Vietnamese arrived at the irrigation ditch. Calley ordered them pushed on top of the mounting pile of bodies, then he and Meadlo shot them. Calley ordered Dursi and Maples to fire, but both refused. Calley then apparently leveled his rifle at Maples, threatening to shoot him if he did not fire, but other soldiers intervened to stop Calley from pulling the trigger.[19] Wounded and panic-stricken, several women and children tried to climb over the bodies and escape the ditch only to be thrown back and shot. Stanley recounted the scene for investigators: "The people in the ditch kept trying to get out and some of them made it to the top, but before they could get away they were shot, too . . . There were a lot of people in the ditch with their heads blown open."[20]

The scene must have exceeded anything these men had ever seen. *Gruesome, macabre,* and other adjectives could not capture the sight of blood, flesh, chips of bone, and bodies convulsing as each bullet struck. The desperate sounds of terrified women screaming to protect their children, the cries of babies, and the horrid moans of the wounded and dying defy description.

By midmorning, members of Charlie Company had killed hundreds of civilians and raped or assaulted countless women and young girls. They encountered no enemy fire and found no weapons in My Lai (4) itself. Despite all of this, Captain Medina radioed the TOC at 0935 hours that his men had killed another sixty-nine Viet Cong, in addition to the fifteen already reported.[21]

Thompson Intervenes

Warrant Officer (WO1) Hugh Thompson and his crew had been flying low over Son My much of the morning. As they flew over the area, they noticed more and more Vietnamese corpses along trails and ditches and the stark lack of American casualties. Following standard procedure, Thompson dropped smoke markers near wounded Vietnamese so that American medics could give them aid. Returning later to these smoke markers, Thompson found soldiers had instead killed the wounded.

Thompson, his crew chief SP4 Glenn Andreotta, and his gunner SP4 Lawrence Colburn spotted a wounded Vietnamese woman and marked her location with smoke. Hovering close, they noticed a squad of American soldiers approaching, one of whom wore the markings of a captain clearly visible to the Bubble crew. Two soldiers on the ground, PFCs Michael Bernhardt and James Flynn, witnessed what Thompson, Andreotta, and Colburn saw from the air. Medina, the soldier with the captain's insignia, inspected the basket the woman had been carrying then nudged her with his boot. Medina claimed she had made a sudden movement, in reaction to which he shot and killed her. Bernhardt maintained that the woman, though wounded and breathing heavily, made no threatening movements. Flynn, however, said that although the woman pretended to be wounded Medina shot and killed her anyway.[22]

Shocked, Thompson flew on. Andreotta soon spotted a canal ditch filled with what appeared from the air to be several wounded Vietnamese. Thompson carefully landed his helicopter close to the ditch and spoke to a nearby sergeant, asking to evacuate the wounded. The sergeant, David Mitchell, replied, "The only way to help them out is to put them out of their misery." A lieutenant, whom Thompson later identified in a lineup as Calley, approached Thompson. Thompson asked "What's going on here?" Calley brusquely told Thompson to mind his own business. Furious, Thompson returned to his helicopter and as he took off Andreotta screamed over the intercom that Mitchell and Calley had begun firing into the ditch, killing the wounded. According to Sledge, Calley complained bitterly about Thompson's interference: "He's not running this show; I'm the boss."[23]

By this time, Thompson had decided he and his crew had to take action. Spotting another bunker filled with Vietnamese, Thompson made a quick pass and noticed a group of soldiers approaching it, clearly with the intent to kill. Thompson landed near enough to block their path. Before leaving his helicopter, Thompson radioed the gunship hovering above, asking its crew to help if things got out of control. He then told Colburn and Andreotta to cover him and open fire if the soldiers fired on him or the men, women, and children.

Thompson told a nearby officer, Lieutenant Brooks, that he intended to take the people out. An annoyed Brooks kept his men at a wary distance. They made no move to stop Thompson and instead sat down to smoke and take a drink from their canteens, further testament to the absence of enemy activity in the area. Thompson coaxed the people out of the bunker and radioed for the gunship hovering above to pick up the Vietnamese. He then returned to the bunker, standing between Brooks's men and the villagers, who surely would have been killed had Thompson not been there. It took the gunship two trips to remove the Vietnamese to a location just southwest of My Lai (4).[24]

Thompson then asked Andreotta and Colburn if they were willing to return to the ditch where they had encountered Calley and Mitchell. Agreeing to take the risk, they turned back. As they made a pass over the ditch, Andreotta thought he saw movement among the mass of over one hundred corpses, many literally shot to pieces. Thompson landed nearby. While he and Colburn stayed with the helicopter, Andreotta inspected the ditch, where he found a small girl of five or six underneath what might have been her dead mother. Andreotta struggled to get the child out of the ditch. Colburn came over to help and was taken aback by the scene—blood, bone, bits of flesh, indistinguishable body parts, and occasional movement and moans of a few but unrecognizable wounded. Fighting their own revulsion and disgust, the three men boarded the helicopter with Colburn holding the little girl in his lap. They flew the girl, who was in shock but amazingly was otherwise unharmed, to an ARVN hospital in Quang Ngai City, then returned to LZ Dottie.[25]

Warrant Officer Hugh Thompson, who, along with crewmates Lawrence Colburn and Glenn Andreotta, intervened to save the lives of Vietnamese civilians at My Lai (4). US Army.

Inside My Lai (4)

Medina and his command group entered the southwest portion of My Lai (4) close behind 3rd Platoon. Bodies of women and children littered the trail. Private Charles Gruver and Sergeant John Smail, both of 3rd Platoon, came across a young boy of about five years of age, who to Smail appeared near death. His hand had been partially shot away and his face had been badly wounded. SP4 Frederick Widmer, a member of Medina's radio team, approached Smail and Gruver standing near the boy. Widmer took an M-16 from someone then fired a short burst into the boy, killing him. Widmer later said that he shot the boy as a mercy killing, claiming if he had not done it someone else eventually would have.[26]

To some of the men in Charlie Company Widmer already had a reputation as a "blood thirsty little joker" who liked to take pictures of dead bodies. Several soldiers claimed they saw Widmer shooting civilians and taking pictures on March 16. Herbert Carter and Harry Stanley observed Widmer shooting the wounded among a mass of about fifty civilians. Carter had already seen enough to make him feel "sick" that morning. He and Stanley had stopped to take a break when Widmer allegedly approached and asked Carter for his .45. Carter handed over the weapon and watched in horror as Widmer started shooting anyone he thought was still alive, including a wounded young boy. Widmer allegedly shot the boy in the neck from a range of just a few feet. The boy tried to get up and walk but after only a few steps fell to the ground, took several deep, labored breaths, then died. According to Stanley, Widmer bragged excitedly, "Did you see that fucker die?" Stanley replied, "I don't see how anyone can just kill a kid."

According to Carter, the pistol jammed after Widmer fired several shots. Frustrated, Widmer handed the weapon back to Carter then walked away. As Carter tried clearing the jammed round, the pistol discharged, wounding him in the foot. Screaming in pain, Carter yelled for a medic. SP5 Abel Flores, one of the Company medics, and Captain Medina quickly arrived to find Stanley already cutting off Carter's boot. Haeberle heard the shot as he stood talking with Jay Roberts, then took several hurried photographs of Medina and Flores attending Carter. Stanley did not actually see the shot but nonetheless told investigators that he thought Carter intentionally shot himself. Carter claimed the wound had been accidental. Several men corroborated Carter's version of the incident. Interestingly, the official wound report described Carter's injury as "GSW [gunshot wound] hostile."[27]

Medina radioed for a medevac to pick up Carter. Upon its arrival Widmer and another soldier carried Carter to the chopper, which took off and apparently radioed Barker to report seeing a large number of bodies on the ground. Barker had to have seen the large groups of bodies from the air, including the mass of corpses not far from where the medevac chopper picked up Carter. SP4 Thomas Kinch and others overheard Barker on the radio asking Medina about the bodies. Medina replied he did not know but would "call forward and find out." Shortly thereafter Medina issued orders to all three platoons to "stop firing."

The wanton slaughter of the villagers of My Lai (4) and other hamlets of Son My also included sexual assaults. An exact number of rapes, forced acts of sodomy, and other similar offenses committed by American soldiers on March 16, 1968, will never be known. That some members of Task Force Barker witnessed, and some committed, such acts cannot be disputed. If descriptions of Charlie Company's history in this regard are accurate, and there is little reason to doubt them, this added brutality to the day's horrifying events should come as no surprise.

One incident in particular shows the difficulty of reconciling accusations to witness testimony. In this case, soldiers allegedly raped a young woman then killed her, but the soldiers who participated in the assault all claim someone else committed the act. SP4 Charles Hutto claimed Sergeants Joe Jolly and Esequiel Torres took turns raping the woman in a hut. Hutto apparently did not see the men kill her but claimed he later heard that one of the soldiers killed the girl. Varnado Simpson claimed Hutto, SP4 Max Hutson, SP4 Floyd Wright, and others violated the woman then shot her. Dean Fields testified that Hutto had "intercourse" with the woman while Wright held her down. Fields said the men did not beat her but that she "wasn't giving herself to the men willingly." SP4 Thomas Partsch of 2nd Platoon testified to investigators that he witnessed the same incident but that Hutto and Hutson committed the assault. Jolly, Wright, and Hutson denied the incident even happened. Holding any of these men responsible for the woman's rape and death proved hopeless.[28]

In another instance, PFCs Leonard Gonzales and Dennis Bunning allegedly saw Sergeant Kenneth Hodges enter a hut with a young girl in Binh Tay. Gonzales did not see Hodges violate her but assumed he did, but Bunning claimed that Hodges raped the girl. According to Bunning, others may have violated the same girl before and after Hodges. Gonzales speculated that sexual assaults occurred throughout My Lai (4) and Binh Tay: "I know there was raping, because anytime we ever did go into a village there's always raping."[29]

From the air, helicopter crews noticed large numbers of bodies strewn across the area and heard Thompson's distressing radio calls. From his helicopter, Chief Warrant Officer (CWO) Dan Millians clearly saw bodies scattered around My Lai (4), including a large group of bodies in a ditch. He later told investigators that the ground assault met no resistance and he saw no bodies until after the troops arrived. While providing air cover for Thompson, WO1 Jerry Culverhouse counted between seventy-five and one hundred bodies in the ditch near Thompson's helicopter and saw a soldier fire into the ditch. First Lieutenant Brian Livingston saw from the air dozens of dead women and children, claiming the "shallow water in the ditch appeared to be red with blood." Private Dale Mott, a door gunner on board one of the Sharks, saw the bodies in the ditch and witnessed soldiers firing into groups of Vietnamese.[30]

Flying above Son My, Colonel Barker's executive officer, Major Charles Calhoun, radioed Medina to stop firing at about 1030 hours. What provoked this order to "stop the killing" is unclear. Calhoun had radioed Medina at least once during the morning, asking about civilian deaths, to which Medina replied that artillery and fire from gunships had killed twenty to twenty-eight civilians. It is also likely that Calhoun had overheard helicopter crews' claims of large numbers of civilians killed, although he later denied this to investigators.

As Charlie Company conducted its part of the operation on March 16, so too did Bravo Company, 4th Battalion, 3rd Infantry carry out its part of the plan in the far east of Son My along the coast of the South China Sea. From the previous night's briefings, Captain Earl Michles, Bravo Company's commander, had made clear to his platoon leaders that this would be a search and destroy operation. Michles told his men that the time had come to "take care of them, to get rid of them," referring to the Viet Cong in Pinkville. No one present at the briefing at LZ Uptight that morning took this to mean killing civilians, even though they all knew many villagers sympathized with the Viet Cong. Michles ordered his men to round up villagers and process them as they always did, reminding them to be careful with civilians and not to shoot livestock belonging to local farmers.

Despite these precautions, allegations surfaced during the Peers investigation that members of Bravo Company's 1st Platoon may have killed over ninety civilians in the hamlet of My Hoi, or My Khe (4) as it was named on American maps. In all, 1st Platoon claimed to have killed thirty-eight Viet Cong in My Khe (4) on March 16. No casualties had been reported, nor had any weapons been captured by 1st Platoon. Later that afternoon, Captain Michles reported to Task Force Barker that the thirty-eight Viet Cong killed did not include any women or children. Others disputed the numbers. SP4 Peter Bretenstein saw a few bodies, mostly on the ridge near the beach but did not "see any thirty-eight anybody." Lieutenant Thomas Willingham's radioman, SP4 Mario Fernandez, claimed that as he and Willingham walked down the main trail he saw at least twenty dead women and children. SP4 Homer Hall, a rifleman in 1st Squad, saw dead women and children in bunkers and along the footpath to the beach. PFC Larry Homes recalled "nearly everyone was firing" at villagers trying to flee toward the beach: "They were running around like crazy people." While he saw no bodies, Private Morris Mitchner said that over eighty people had been killed, most in their bunkers by explosives thrown in by the point team and some soldiers of 1st Squad. Sergeant Henry Cardines, the weapons squad leader, saw unburied bodies of women and children when 1st Platoon came back through My Khe (4) the next day.

Night

At about 1330 hours on March 16 Charlie Company moved on to My Lai (1), where soldiers rounded up approximately seventy more villagers. After detaining several military-aged males among the group, they sent the remaining men, women, and children on to Quang Ngai City. Charlie Company continued burning hootches and destroying suspected bunkers and by late afternoon had linked with Bravo Company at the planned night defensive position.

As the companies readied their positions for the night, a helicopter carrying Captain Kotouc and several Vietnamese National Police arrived to interrogate suspected Viet Cong brought in by both Charlie and Bravo Companies. Kotouc and Medina needed to know the locations of minefields and booby traps for Task Force Barker's movements the next day. Of the twelve or so prisoners, police quickly identified three as Viet Cong. Captain Kotouc began questioning one of the men through Medina's interpreter, Sergeant Nguyen Dinh Phu, while police watched over the others, who squatted bound and blindfolded in a line. Medina, Kotouc's interpreter Sergeant Do Thanh Hien, and several others watched uneasily from nearby. Vietnamese National Police did not fall under American command, thus American officers in the field had to do a delicate dance to maintain good working relations with Vietnamese agencies. Working with Vietnamese National Police could be difficult, as they could be excessively brutal toward prisoners, using torture and even execution to get desired information.

Getting no results, Kotouc took aside the Viet Cong suspect, identified as a hamlet chief, and forced him to kneel. He then took out a large knife and waved it in front of the man's face, threatening to cut off one of his fingers if he did not talk. Kotouc repeatedly hit the man's outstretched fingers with the blunt edge of his knife, then allegedly cut off part of the man's little finger of his right hand, after which he put the blade to the man's neck, making a long but light cut. Still, the man refused to talk. PFC James Flynn, the forward observer for the mortar platoon, witnessed the incident from just a few feet away.

Hien then questioned the man for another twenty minutes. Though he was clearly frightened and his hand bloodied, the hamlet chief remained obstinate. Hien began to doubt the man was really Viet Cong, but the police insisted and in their impatience convinced Hien to ask Kotouc if they could kill him. Kotouc purportedly replied, "Okay," then "signaled to the man that his spirit was going up to heaven." The police took the man to a nearby shallow ditch, where with five quick shots they killed him. The police took a second Viet Cong to the same place, perhaps to frighten the suspect into talking by showing him the now-dead chief. Without asking anyone's permission, the police shot and killed this second man in short order. SP4 Charles West claimed the police shot eight to ten Viet Cong suspects before one finally told his interrogators that the 48th Local Force Battalion had left the area the previous night. Lieutenant Roger Alaux, the forward artillery observer who also witnessed the incident, told investigators that the prisoners had been "shot down in cold blood after a kangaroo court." Captain Medina stepped in to prevent the police from killing the remaining prisoners, telling them to "stop this, that this was not supposed to be going on." Hien and SP4 John Paul, one of Medina's radiomen, went to the ditch to inspect the bodies, noting the police had shot the suspects execution-style. Accepting the "common practice" of National Police to kill prisoners, Medina did not report the shooting.[31]

Calley and Charlie Company's 1st Platoon set up a security position some eight hundred meters to the southwest of the night laager site occupied by Charlie and Bravo Companies. Men of both companies now found themselves spending the night in and around a cemetery. Thomas Partsch, of Charlie Company's 2nd Platoon, enjoyed hot chow with "pop and beer," then wrote an entry in his diary before an hour-and-a-half stint on guard duty that night: "We started to move slowly through the village shooting everything in sight children men and women and animals. Some was sickening. There [*sic*] legs were shot off and they were still moving. It was just hanging there. I think their bodies were made of rubber. I didn't fire a round yet and couldn't kill anybody not even a chicken. I couldn't . . . We killed about 100 people. After a while they said not to kill women and children."[32]

One of the helicopter pilots, Lieutenant Brian Livingston, wrote his wife, Betz, that day, telling her what he had seen from the air: "Well it's been a long day, some nasty sights. I saw the insertion of infantrymen and they were animals . . . I've never seen so many people dead in one spot. Ninety-five percent were women and kids. A captain walked up to this little girl, he turned away took five steps, and fired a volley of shots into her. This Negro sergeant started shooting people in the head . . . I'll tell you something it sure makes one wonder why we are here."[33]

3 Aftermath

I would like to pass on the following message from Gen. Westmoreland: OP Muscatine contact northeast of Quang Ngai City on 16 March dealt enemy a heavy blow. Congratulations to officers and men of C/1-20 INF and B/4-3 INF for outstanding action. I add my congratulations for the teamwork and aggressiveness exhibited by the above-mentioned companies and to all others participating in this operation.

Major General Samuel W. Koster, Commanding General, Americal Division

At day's end, Task Force Barker claimed 128 Viet Cong killed, three weapons captured, an assortment of equipment and food caches secured or destroyed, and numerous buildings and other structures razed in the Son My operation. This tally of supposed destruction inflicted upon the enemy came at the modest cost of two American dead and eleven wounded, including Herbert Carter's accidental wound. With the exception of Carter, Charlie Company's only casualty, mines or booby traps had caused all of the American casualties. Direct enemy fire had not killed or wounded anyone. Charlie Company did report the death of "approximately 10–11 women and children art[iller]y or gunships. These were not included in the body count."[1] In reality, as many as five hundred men, women, and children had been killed.

For the villagers of Son My, March 16 had been a day of unimaginable fear and horror. Do Ba, who when the shelling began hid in a shelter near his house, survived the shooting. Soldiers from Charlie Company approached his home and shot his family's two cows then seized him. Detained with several others, Do Ba saw several corpses as "a soldier" took him to a ditch, where he sat for over half an hour alongside what he estimated to be over one hundred of his neighbors. "After that we were shot," he later told investigators. Somehow, the spray of bullets only wounded Do Ba in the neck and hand. He quickly lost consciousness and next remembered being taken along Route 521 to a hospital in Truong An, where he remained for two months. His mother, Nguyen Thi Thi, hid in another shelter with his three sisters, who had been on their way home from an overnight stay with friends. They remained hidden until they found a safe moment to flee. Do Ba did not know their fate, nor did his mother and sisters know his, until several days later, when his mother found him in the hospital at Truong An.[2]

Pham Thua saw a group of soldiers shoot several villagers on the southeastern edge of Binh Tay and claimed seven black soldiers raped a woman in the hamlet. Soldiers gathered a large group of about two hundred villagers, whom he feared would be shot, but other soldiers intervened and moved the villagers out of the area. He witnessed soldiers shoot his family's livestock and burn his home to the ground. In My Lai (4), Pham Lai fled after remaining hidden with twelve others until the soldiers finished burning homes and shooting livestock. He and others returned later in the afternoon to find utter devastation. Homes lay in ashes and bodies littered the trails. He helped bury several women and children and then tended to members of his own family who had been killed. With no shelter, he and others built crude bamboo huts to pass the night.

Nguyen Thi Nhung stayed in the water in the rice field for almost three hours. She finally left her hiding place in the late morning and approached My Lai (4) on a path littered with bodies. Hearing shots in the village she fled toward Truong An. She returned in the afternoon to find her home destroyed and livestock killed. As she and other survivors searched the ditches filled with corpses, she found her younger brother, four of her sisters, a sister-in-law, and nine nieces and nephews dead. Her mother and father had also been killed. Neighbors from the adjoining villages helped her and other villagers bury their dead.

Pham Thi Don managed to escape unharmed. Soldiers came to her house and forced her, her father, her two sisters-in-law, and her three nephews outside. Her two brothers-in-law had already left home to work in the fields when the shelling began. As soldiers herded her family toward an irrigation ditch, she slipped back and then hid among some bushes. Unnoticed, she fled toward Son Hoa, where she found her daughter, who had left earlier in the morning. On their return to My Lai (4) later that day, they met neighbors and other villagers, who told them that Americans had shot and killed many in the village. She and her daughter searched among the bodies and finally found her father, her two sisters-in-law, and her three nephews in the irrigation ditch. The two brothers-in-law had escaped and later returned to help bury their families.[3]

Le Thi Em and her family had stayed in their home when the shelling began that morning. Soldiers took her and her two sons, ages six and ten, from the home and placed them among a larger group of villagers. Near a rice field next to the main trail, she claimed, a soldier took an elderly couple and a younger man and his small son, forced them to lie down, and shot them. Other soldiers then turned their rifles on the group. She and her two sons fell to the ground and pretended to be shot. Waiting until the soldiers left, they escaped to Son Hoa. Later that day, she returned to find her aunt and uncle, two cousins, and three of her cousins' children killed.[4]

Le Tong fared much better than most of his neighbors. He and his family had been hiding in a bunker in a bamboo thicket near his family home for over an hour when soldiers pulled them out and sent them away toward Binh Dong. He and his family returned to My Lai (4) that afternoon to find their home completely burned and their three pigs shot dead. Incredibly he and his family survived the horrific day without a scratch.

Operations March 17–19

On the surface, Task Force Barker carried on as if the chilling events of March 16 had never happened, but a scratch beneath would reveal that something terribly wrong had occurred. On the morning of March 17, Charlie and Bravo Companies continued operations southward along the coast. Though not in force, several Viet Cong still operated in the area. Booby traps and mines made movement along roads and trails particularly dangerous. Task Force Barker's extended area of operations remained hostile and deadly.

Captain Medina led Charlie Company south from its night defensive position, just inland from the coast. Charlie Company's objectives for the day included destroying the hamlets of My Khe (3), My Khe (1), and My Khe (2), which lay mostly deserted in a rough line north-to-south to where the Tra Khuc River intersected a coastal channel. After searching the hamlets and burning houses and other structures, Charlie Company returned northward to establish a night defensive position just south of the one it had occupied the night of March 16. As the Company moved out that morning, the warm humid air revealed the repulsive odor of fresh shallow graves, noticeable to several of the men of Charlie Company as they passed within a few hundred meters of My Lai (4).

Captain Medina, worried about Viet Cong hitting the Company from the rear, needed an observation post. Hill 85, so named on maps because of its height in meters, stood about a thousand meters along Charlie Company's path to provide an excellent vantage point of the surrounding area. Medina knew the top of the hill would likely be mined and that booby traps would litter the approaches. The previous day's aerial reconnaissance confirmed Viet Cong activity on the hill by discovering several 60mm mortar rounds on the hillside. Calley's 1st Platoon began ascending Hill 85 with orders not to go all the way to the top. From midway up the hill, 1st Platoon could keep watch as the rest of Charlie Company continued southward and also alert Bravo Company of any movement as it patrolled to the east along the coastline. As 1st Platoon advanced up the hill, the soldiers could see smoke still rising from My Lai (4).

Paul Meadlo, operating the minesweeper, cleared a path up the hill to the observation point, which they reached without incident. As Meadlo led the remainder of the men back down the hill, Lieutenant Calley ordered him to stop sweeping for mines to speed up their pace. After only a few yards Meadlo stepped on a mine. Shrapnel from the explosion blew off Meadlo's foot and slightly wounded Calley in the neck and face. Calley refused evacuation and received treatment for his wounds in the field. Meadlo, however, needed immediate medical attention, which SP4 Robert Lee, the 1st Platoon medic, provided. As he waited for the medevac helicopter, Meadlo reportedly yelled to Calley that God had punished him for what he had done the previous day: "You got yours coming!" Lee vividly recalled how Meadlo kept repeating that God would punish Calley for what he had made him do. Meadlo could not recall saying anything to that effect, admitting that he "was so full of pain that I don't remember what I did say."[5]

After the explosion Medina ordered 1st Platoon to abandon Hill 85 and rejoin Charlie Company near My Khe (1), hoping to avoid more casualties. Throughout the morning and early afternoon Charlie Company moved southward, burning hootches and other structures in its path. For the most part villagers had deserted the area. As 2nd and 3rd Platoons swept through the hamlets, they flushed out two Viet Cong, killing both as they tried to run away. Medina had 1st Platoon hang back a short distance to seize any Viet Cong attempting to escape rearward. The tactic paid off, as 1st Platoon caught four suspected Viet Cong just outside of My Khe (2) at around 1530 hours that afternoon.

Captain Medina and his Vietnamese interpreter, Sergeant Phu, began interrogating the two teenage boys, an older man, and a woman who "was acting like she was out of her mind and she was kind of bubbling at the mouth." An ammonia capsule brought the woman back to full consciousness, though Medina and the medic attending her believed it all an act. The woman had no blouse, so Medina took the shirt from one of the male suspects for her to cover herself. Two of the male suspects appeared to be local Viet Cong, but the third, whom Medina referred to as "an executive-looking individual," clearly did not fit the general description of a local. His dress and manner indicated that he held high rank and came from somewhere else. As they questioned one of the other suspected Viet Cong, the "executive-looking" man shouted a command to the others. Medina struck him across the face with the back of his hand, causing a bloody cut on the man's forehead.

Both Medina and Sergeant Phu believed they had captured an important Viet Cong officer but wanted to get him talking before handing him over to the National Police, whom Medina feared would abruptly kill him. Medina, who had earlier emptied the bullets from his revolver, then pretended to load the weapon with a single round. He placed the gun to the man's head, but the man saw through the ruse and refused to talk. Medina then had Phu place the man against a nearby coconut tree. Medina stood about fifteen meters away, raised his M-16, and fired a shot into the tree several inches above the man's head. Though shaken the man remained silent. Medina then fired another round, this time just a few inches above the Viet Cong's head. Medina drew close to the man's face and pointed at the first two bullet holes, then placed his finger between the man's eyes, indicating where the next shot would strike. When he backed up and raised the weapon as if to fire a third and final shot, the man began talking.

Medina later claimed he would not have killed the man "in cold blood."

The man proved indeed to be a "high-ranking" Viet Cong official, actually the province chief for the Viet Cong in Quang Ngai. He told Medina that the 48th Local Force Battalion had left the area before March 16 and that the Viet Cong had used My Lai (4) as a triage area for their wounded, hiding them during the day and moving them out of the area at night to hospital camps. Medina apparently posed for a picture with his prize catch, holding a long knife to the man's throat while drinking from a freshly cut coconut.[6]

The woman claimed to have been pressed into a Viet Cong medical unit. Although Medina later denied that he knew why she had no blouse, others claimed Medina should have known. Gregory Olsen saw a GI ("government issue," a World War II term for an American soldier) pull the woman from a hut, rip off her blouse, and carry her over his shoulder as he loudly boasted he would rape her. Dennis Conti apparently "inspected" the woman, did not like what he saw, and told those gathered around to think twice about having their turn with her. Thomas Kinch, of Charlie Company's weapons platoon, saw the same GI, whom he identified as Daniel Simone, bring her to Medina, again carrying her over his shoulder. Kinch believed Medina should have known Simone's intent.[7]

A helicopter arrived to pick up the Viet Cong suspects, then Medina and Charlie Company returned north to establish a night defensive position just east of My Khe (1). Along the way Medina reported one additional Viet Cong killed in a bunker. By 1800 hours Charlie Company had set up its defensive position and fortified for the night.

On March 18 Charlie Company began moving toward its pick-up zone near My Lai (3). A booby trap wounded two more GIs as the Company moved through My Lai (1). As Charlie Company neared My Lai (3) Medina received word by radio that Colonel Oran Henderson, the commander of the 11th Infantry Brigade, wanted to speak with him. A helicopter delivered Henderson and the 11th Infantry Brigade S-2, Lieutenant Colonel Richard Blackledge, to the pick-up zone. According to Medina, he and Henderson spoke for about half an hour, during which Henderson told Medina that he had received reports of unnecessary killings at My Lai (4) and that a helicopter pilot had reported that Medina had killed a "female noncombatant." Medina explained the circumstances surrounding his shooting of the woman, which Henderson found "understandable." As for large numbers of women and children killed in My Lai (4), Medina said that he had no knowledge of any such reports and that he found it hard to believe that "American soldiers could do such a thing." Henderson recalled Medina then telling him that he had already reported to Lieutenant Colonel Frank Barker that twenty civilian casualties had been "unavoidable" and that to the best of his knowledge Charlie Company had not committed any unnecessary killings. Henderson informed Medina that he had ordered an investigation. Charlie Company then returned to LZ Dottie, completing its part of the operation.

In the weeks that followed, Charlie Company patrolled and provided security for LZ Dottie. On April 8, Charlie Company returned to its own battalion, the 1st Battalion of the 20th Infantry, near Quang Ngai City. On April 7, the Americal Division issued a brief order: "Task Force Barker discontinues operations in Muscatine AO and is disbanded effective 081200H APR 68."[8]

Initial Reports

Reports and other indications that something wrong had occurred on March 16 quickly surfaced at a variety of command levels. The incident itself seemed so bizarre that some found the story difficult to take seriously, while others who knew something had happened were divided between a few who wanted justice and many who either wanted to cover it up or simply ignore it.[9]

After landing his helicopter to refuel at LZ Dottie at about 1100 hours on March 16, WO1 Hugh Thompson, along with several other pilots and crewmembers, sought his section leader, Lieutenant Barry Lloyd, to report "unnecessary killing" in My Lai (4). Lloyd had no doubt as to Thompson's anger, but at first he thought Thompson, who had not been with the unit long, had exaggerated the situation. After speaking with other pilots, however, Lloyd came to believe the reports. Lloyd and Thompson went to see Major Frederic Watke, the commander of Bravo Company, 123rd Aviation Battalion, in the operations center, where Thompson laid out what he and his crew had seen, describing to Watke "rice paddies red with blood." Struggling to control his emotions, Thompson described landing his ship to prevent soldiers on the ground from killing a group of women and children. As he overheard Thompson and others describe what happened in and around My Lai (4), Sergeant Lawrence Kubert, who ran the operations center, recalled having a distinct feeling that "something bad had happened, something bad."

With some skepticism Watke listened to Thompson and other pilots tell their story. He, too, initially worried that Thompson and his fellow pilots "were over-dramatizing" what they had seen, assuming "his people's" lack of combat experience had led them to "exaggerate" the situation. Still, the reports indicated that noncombatants, including children, had possibly been the victim of "unnecessary" and "needless" killing. Watke did not immediately relay Thompson's very serious charges to Lieutenant Colonel Barker, delaying more than half an hour before walking over to the nearby Task Force TOC. Thompson's contention that he had landed to stop soldiers on the ground from shooting people he determined to be noncombatants concerned Watke, lest charges of interfering with a combat operation be brought against his company, allegations that could derail a major's chances of promotion. Later that day Thompson completed an after-action report on which Lieutenant Lloyd wrote "NOTICE" in the margin where Thompson alleged ground units had engaged in "needless shooting" of civilians. Investigators later could not locate the original, or any, copy of Thompson's after-action report.

Watke verbally relayed to Barker what Thompson and others had alleged, including Thompson's confrontation with the men on the ground. He recalled Barker reacting with "concern" though not surprise. Barker radioed Major Charles Calhoun, who had remained above Son My monitoring the operation from the air, to check with Captain Medina on the ground about unnecessary killing of noncombatants, then to return to LZ Dottie so that Barker could fly over the area himself. For his part Watke believed he had done the proper thing. Now the matter lay in Barker's hands, as Barker commanded the Task Force and had the authority to intervene during the operation, if warranted.

Later in the afternoon Watke again saw Barker at the Task Force TOC. Barker apparently told Watke that he had checked with Captain Medina and found that indeed some civilians had unfortunately been killed but discovered nothing to substantiate the claims of Watke's pilots, including the confrontation between Thompson and members of Charlie Company. Watke "didn't believe" Barker, and that evening he went to his immediate superior, Lieutenant Colonel John Holladay, commander of the 123rd Aviation Battalion. Although troubled, Holladay warned Watke to be sure about the allegations, because if wrong Watke's military career, if not Holladay's chance at promotion, could be irrevocably harmed. Watke felt obligated to send the report forward; that way, at least, no one could come back later and accuse him of negligence, or so he thought. Holladay recalled "agonizing" over what he first thought "was an almost unbelievable story," finding it difficult to "absorb" what Watke had told him. Holladay then decided to approach Brigadier General George Young, the assistant commander of the Americal Division, first thing in the morning.

At LZ Dottie the 11th Infantry Brigade's correspondent, Jay Roberts, who had seen killing in My Lai (4) that morning, had to submit a story about the operation for the Brigade's press release. After returning to LZ Dottie early in the afternoon, Roberts bumped into Lieutenant Colonel Barker near the Task Force TOC and asked about the status of the day's operations. According to Roberts, Barker seemed open to talking and invited Roberts into the TOC, where he gave Roberts a quick update. Roberts asked about the high kill count versus the low number of weapons captured, to which Barker replied, "Don't worry about it," telling Roberts to write a "good story" on Task Force Barker. Roberts knew what had happened at My Lai (4) but did not want to "stir up any scandal . . . We just wanted to write a story and do our jobs."

That evening, the regularly scheduled Americal Division daily briefing took place in Chu Lai, and both Brigadier General Young and Major General Samuel Koster attended. As many as fifty officers gathered to hear that units of the Americal Division had killed 138 Viet Cong the previous day, with Task Force Barker accounting for 128. Despite 128 kills, Task Force Barker captured only three weapons. Among those attending the briefing, several speculated that Task Force Barker had lied, believing the figure of 128 to be far too high for just three weapons captured. Lieutenant Colonel Francis Lewis, the Americal Division chaplain, recalled that the announcement of the body count and the low weapons count caused audible "murmuring" in the briefing room. According to Lewis it was "common knowledge" that "something had gone wrong," though not in the form of an atrocity but rather a "combat mistake." Major General Koster's aide, Captain Daniel Roberts, recalled walking behind Brigadier General Young and Koster as they left the briefing when a clearly agitated Koster told an "annoyed" Young to check the report to rectify the disparity.

On Sunday, March 17, Hugh Thompson visited Captain Carl Creswell, a chaplain in the Americal Division, to retell his story. Creswell noted that Thompson remained extremely "upset" about what he had seen the previous day and advised Thompson to report it through official channels, which by this point Thompson had already done. For his part, Creswell relayed Thompson's story to his superior, Lieutenant Colonel Lewis, who had already heard rumors that civilians had been killed at My Lai (4). Lewis promised to pursue Thompson's report but delayed doing so because the Division operations officer, Colonel Jesmond Balmer, happened to be on leave at the time.[10]

On that same morning Holladay and Watke met with Brigadier General Young at 0800 hours in Chu Lai. Watke informed Young of the shootings at the ditch, the confrontation between Thompson and Charlie Company, and the large number of bodies seen from the air. Young recalled only that Watke related a confrontation between Thompson and ground troops over civilians caught in a cross fire but denied knowing about mass indiscriminate killings. Both Watke and Holladay later noted that Young had not been surprised at the allegation that unnecessary killings had occurred at My Lai (4). Thompson's story had now gone forward in three different channels.

According to the Peers Inquiry report, Young then informed the commander of the Americal Division, Major General Koster, who had also been in the air over Son My on March 16. Both Young and Koster denied discussing specific incidents reported earlier by Watke. According to Koster the two instead focused on the confrontation between air and ground units and the possibility that ground troops "endangered civilians by firing more than the circumstances required." Young somehow concluded that inadvertent cross fire caused unnecessary killings at My Lai (4) rather than that Thompson had landed to prevent troops on the ground from killing noncombatants. Koster left the meeting with the same impression and later denied being told by Young or anyone else that American troops had intentionally killed noncombatants, though in an interview with CID investigators he admitted that Young may have told him about indiscriminate killings. Already aware from both Captain Medina and Colonel Henderson that some civilians had been killed, Koster ordered Young to "find out what went on down there . . . let's have the facts."[11]

Young flew to LZ Dottie on late Sunday afternoon to talk with Major Charles Calhoun, Task Force Barker's executive officer. As they flew to LZ Dottie, Young's staff clearly recalled that the sky to the east of the LZ remained shrouded in heavy smoke from fires still smoldering in Son My. Calhoun gave Young a quick rundown on Task Force Barker's operations on March 16, telling him that, of the 128 Viet Cong dead, artillery fire had killed sixty-nine. Of these, said Calhoun, some might have been civilians. Young accepted Calhoun's briefing without comment.

On the morning of Monday, March 18, Young met with Colonel Henderson, Lieutenant Colonel Barker, Lieutenant Colonel Holladay, and Major Watke at LZ Dottie. Young supposedly warned the four officers, "We are the only five that know about this . . . Something happened yesterday." He then allowed Watke to repeat the story now for the third time. Watke did not overtly suggest that cross fire had caused noncombatant casualties. Young told Colonel Henderson, "I want you to investigate this" and requested a report within seventy-two hours. Young apparently did not specify how Henderson should submit the report or if he should include sworn testimony. Of the five present all but Holladay had flown over My Lai (4) at some point on March 16.

Inadequate Investigations

On March 18, Colonel Henderson began a probe that the Peers Inquiry later described as "little more than a pretense . . . subsequently misrepresented as a thorough investigation." Henderson first interviewed Hugh Thompson, Jerry Culverhouse, and Lawrence Colburn. Henderson recalled speaking only with Thompson, who retold his story of seeing bodies along trails and in a ditch, a captain shooting a woman at close range, and Charlie Company's "extremely wild shooting" in and around My Lai (4). Henderson claimed Thompson said nothing about ground troops shooting women and children in a ditch or of landing his helicopter to prevent soldiers from killing a group of civilian noncombatants. Thompson, Culverhouse, and Colburn, however, each recalled telling Henderson in detail what they witnessed and what they did the morning of March 16, including seeing masses of bodies. Culverhouse remembered specifically that Henderson clearly appeared "uneasy" as he described the "blood actually running off from the bodies down into the ditch." Henderson did not place any of the three under oath, nor did he have them sign a written statement.

After talking with Thompson and his crew, Henderson flew out to confer with Captain Medina about his alleged killing of the woman and inquire, again, about noncombatant casualties, as Charlie Company prepared to return to LZ Dottie. As previously described Medina explained how and why he shot the woman, an explanation that apparently satisfied Henderson. Medina also repeated that he had seen twenty to twenty-eight civilian casualties, all of which he attributed to artillery or gunship fire. Henderson recalled that at this point he ordered Medina and Charlie Company to return to My Lai (4) to account for all of the casualties, an order that Major General Koster countermanded. However, Henderson actually gave the order that Koster countermanded on the afternoon of March 16, not March 18. Lieutenant Colonel Godfrey Crowe, the 11th Infantry Brigade S-3, and Major Calhoun corroborated Medina's recollection that the countermanded order had taken place on the afternoon of the 16th rather than the 18th.

Henderson did not place Medina under oath or collect a signed statement. Even Lieutenant Colonel Blackledge, who accompanied Henderson to the field to meet with Medina, later claimed ignorance of the true purpose of Henderson's visit. Blackledge rarely went out into the field, suggesting to the Peers Inquiry that his presence served as a "little CYA operation" to prove that Henderson had indeed done due diligence by talking with Medina.

Henderson then flew to LZ Dottie to meet troops of Charlie Company as they returned from the field. In what the Peers Inquiry later described as a "totally meaningless action," Henderson gathered a few dozen men of Charlie Company to ask them about March 16. Henderson first told them that as the new Brigade commander he wanted to thank them for doing a "damn fine job" on the operation. He then revealed that "unsubstantiated reports" alleged that Charlie Company killed some civilian noncombatants during the operation, which if true "would certainly discolor the fine record that they had." Henderson asked them collectively if anyone had "observed any acts against noncombatants, any wild shooting? Did any of you, or do you have knowledge of anybody killing any civilians during this operation?" In response, he "got silence." He then pointed to three or four individual soldiers, asking them directly the same question, getting a "loud, clear response 'No, sir!'" When asked directly by Henderson if Charlie Company had "conducted" itself in such a way that "the Vietnamese will think we are their friends," Sergeant Jay Buchanan of 2nd Platoon replied, "I have no comment, sir." Sergeant Isaiah Cowan of 1st Platoon recalled that, after Henderson asked if anything "unusual" had occurred on the operation, they collectively responded "no comment" then "moved on." According to Henderson, "The men had their heads held high," none tried to "ignore my eyes," and all seemed in "high spirits." To Henderson the men of Charlie Company did not appear "to be a bunch of soldiers who had just gone out and shot up the countryside and killed a bunch of women and children." Again, Henderson required no oath, nor did he or his staff take any signed statements, nor did he want any blemish so early in his command of the 11th Infantry Brigade.

In the meantime Lieutenant Colonel Barker directed Captain Medina to look into the allegation made by Thompson and others that a "colored" NCO had shot several civilians in a ditch. Medina first asked Charlie Company's platoon leaders if they had seen or heard that such an incident occurred, to which they replied they had not. Medina sought out Sergeant David Mitchell, a "negro" NCO who led 1st Squad of 1st Platoon. He denied knowing anything about the incident, while, according to Medina, growing increasingly defensive about being singled out: "He said it could have been any colored sergeant, so why was I picking on him?" Medina told him to "forget about it . . . I'm not accusing you of anything or anything like that." Mitchell had no recollection of Medina or anyone else questioning him. Medina then reported to Barker that he had found nothing to substantiate the claim; however, he had heard that a helicopter pilot had made a similar charge and suggested that Barker assign someone "other than myself" to conduct an investigation. According to Medina, Barker replied, "Ernie, you have been doing a real fine job. Go on back to the company and just continue doing the real fine work that you have done."

Following Barker's direction Medina then gathered the Company and informed the men of a probe into various allegations that atrocities may have been committed during the March 16 operation, telling them not to discuss the investigation or the operation among themselves or with anyone else other than their interviewers. Members of Charlie Company, however, remembered Medina's counsel differently. Michael Bernhardt remembered Medina telling the men that he "would back up anybody who was going to get in any trouble for this." Thomas Kinch recalled Medina saying to them, "As far as anyone knows, we went in there, we caught fire, and we returned fire." Thomas Partsch remembered squad leaders telling everyone, "There may be an investigation on this mission, and we were told not to say anything."

Afterward, someone told Medina that Bernhardt threatened to write his congressman about what had happened in My Lai (4). Medina found Bernhardt and asked him to reconsider because of the ongoing inquiry, that "it wouldn't help anything." Bernhardt, who had previously written his congressman to complain about supplies and rations, followed Medina's advice. For the remainder of his tour in Vietnam after March 18, Medina claimed, no one, officially or otherwise, again asked him about My Lai (4).[12]

Colonel Henderson also claimed that he ordered Major Glenn Gibson, commander of the 174th Aviation Company, to ask his pilots if they had any evidence or knowledge of "wild shooting" and unwarranted killing by ground forces on March 16. Henderson testified that Gibson reported that he had spoken with each pilot on the evening of March 18 and none witnessed the killing of noncombatants by ground troops or helicopter gunships. Major Gibson, however, could not recall receiving such an order, nor did he recall discussing the March 16 operation with Colonel Henderson.

On March 19 Henderson informed Brigadier General Young that he had completed his inquiry. Young accepted Henderson's oral account and told him to report to Major General Koster the next day. Both Young and Koster later recalled that Henderson's report came in a series of "conversations" that both Henderson and Young had with Koster, a point that revealed to investigators that both Young and Koster might have assumed the other had responsibility for looking into the allegations; subsequently, neither took the initiative to pursue a formal inquiry. Henderson recalled meeting with Koster on the morning of March 20 to deliver an oral report of his findings. He confirmed previous reports that twenty civilians had been killed during the operation and stated that Captain Medina had provided a satisfactory explanation for shooting the woman, that he could not substantiate claims of indiscriminate killing by ground troops, and that the "confrontation" between Thompson and members of Charlie Company on the ground "had been put to bed." Henderson told Koster that of the dozens of men involved in the March 16 operation he could find only one person, Thompson, willing to claim to have witnessed something out of the ordinary. Once again, Henderson, Young, and Koster thought it unnecessary to produce a written report.

Henderson heard nothing further about his report or the allegations until about two weeks later, when Koster finally requested a written version of the report from March 20. Henderson claimed to have then submitted to Major General Koster on April 4 a multipage report taken from his personal notes from his talks with Thompson, Medina, and others. Henderson claimed further that he placed a copy in the 11th Infantry Brigade headquarters' safe and that Young also acknowledged receiving the report. Young later denied seeing it, and Koster denied requesting it from Colonel Henderson. Captain James Henderson, who worked in the 11th Infantry Brigade TOC, recalled seeing a one-page summary of allegations made by helicopter pilots concerning the operation of March 16–18, but investigators could later locate neither the original nor any copies.

On March 28, Lieutenant Colonel Barker submitted his after-action report to Colonel Henderson. The report did not cover March 17–19, nor did it cover the entire twenty-four hours of March 16, focusing instead on about ten hours from the early morning until midafternoon. Barker explained that, although intelligence indicated that "one local force battalion" operated around My Lai (4) during the operation on the 16th, "it was estimated that only two local force companies supported by two to three local guerrilla platoons opposed the friendly forces." He claimed that artillery had killed sixty-eight Viet Cong during the "initial preparation." As Charlie Company moved into My Lai (4), the Viet Cong responded with "small arms fire." Bravo Company accounted for thirty Viet Cong killed after engaging "one enemy platoon," and both companies "received sporadic sniper fire and encountered numerous enemy booby traps." Barker reported 128 Viet Cong killed and eleven captured and listed captured equipment, including the three rifles, all against only two Americans killed and eleven wounded. Barker's "commander analysis" concluded: "This operation was well planned, well executed, and successful. Friendly casualties were light and the enemy suffered heavily. On this operation the civilian population supporting the VC in the area numbered approximately 200. This created a problem in population control and medical care of those civilians caught in the fire of the opposing forces. However, the infantry units on the ground and helicopters were able to assist civilians in leaving the area and in caring for and/or evacuating the wounded."[13]

Meanwhile, Jay Roberts's embellished press release quickly found its way up MACV's public relations chain and onto newsprint in Vietnam and the United States. Roberts quoted Barker's assessment of the day's battle: "The combat assault went like clockwork."[14] The Americal Division's *News Sheet* for March 18 hailed the exploits of "Barker's Bastards," while *Stars and Stripes* described "heavy fighting" in a "bloody day-long battle" with Viet Cong units of "unknown" size in Quang Ngai Province, resulting in 128 Viet Cong killed.[15] The kill count even made the front page of the *New York Times,* which reported, "American troops caught a North Vietnamese force in a pincer movement" near the coast in Quang Ngai Province, "killing 128 enemy soldiers in daylong fighting." Interestingly, the *New York Times* piece noted, "It was not made clear how many of the enemy had been killed by the artillery and helicopter attacks, and how many were shot down by the American infantrymen."[16]

Vietnamese Reports and Viet Cong "Propaganda"

Reports from villagers in the Son My area and from Viet Cong propaganda that mass numbers of civilians had been killed during an American combat operation surfaced almost immediately. Village and district officials also received and submitted various reports about the operation in Son My. How American and Vietnamese officials considered these followed a similar pattern as the initial inquiries conducted within Task Force Barker. Because of accounts that relied upon incomplete or misleading information, some officials may not have realized an atrocity had even occurred. Memories conflict over who received what report, if any was received at all, and when. The confusion likely convinced or forced Major General Koster to require a written report from Colonel Henderson.

Perhaps the earliest report to come through official South Vietnamese government channels came from the Census Grievance Committee representative in Son My. Covertly funded by the Central Intelligence Agency (CIA), the Census Grievance Committee program provided a means for villagers to file complaints against the government. It may also have provided information on suspected Viet Cong, thus the CIA's support of the program. The brief report described an operation "conducted by allied forces" on March 15 in Tu Cung hamlet, which included My Lai (4). Clearly, it referred to March 16 rather than March 15, as no operations occurred in the area on the 15th. The report claimed that during a "fierce battle" between allied forces and local Viet Cong 320 people had been killed in Thuan Yen and Binh Dong, 27 killed at My Lai, and 80 killed at Co Luy. The 427 dead included Viet Cong but also "young and old" villagers. Dated 1600 hours on March 18, the report did not explicitly allege wrongful killing. The head of the Census Grievance Committee for Quang Ngai Province, Nguyen Tuc Te, and his assistant Ta Linh Vien, later denied receiving such a report but did admit to investigators that they had received several verbal accounts suggesting that large numbers of people, including both Viet Cong and villagers, had been killed in the Son My area on March 16. They did not conduct an onsite investigation, because in their opinion the Viet Cong still controlled the area.[17]

Lieutenant Colonel William Guinn, the deputy province advisor for Quang Ngai, received a translation of the report, which he found transcribed so poorly he "could hardly read it." Disbelieving the high number of killed but accepting the report's premise that the casualties had been caused by "an act of war" in a "free-fire zone," Guinn "didn't consider it a war crime" because of when and where the operation took place. While Guinn claimed to have forwarded the report to Henderson at 11th Infantry Brigade headquarters in Duc Pho, he did not pursue the matter within his own chain of command. Henderson claimed he did not receive any reports from Guinn.

Beginning late in the day on the 16th, Do Dinh Luyen, the village chief of Son My, heard "rumors on the street" about Task Force Barker's sweep through Son My. On March 22, he submitted a written report to his superior, Lieutenant Tran Ngoc Tan, the chief for Son Tinh District, specifying that one American soldier had been killed and another two wounded, against forty-eight Viet Cong killed and fifty-two wounded, and most significantly that 570 civilians had been killed—480 in My Lai (4) and at least 90 in My Khe (4). Do Dinh Luyen later downplayed this initial report as information gathered from Viet Cong propaganda. He claimed to have reported only 30 civilian deaths, while the Viet Cong dead numbered in the hundreds. His actual written report did not delineate fact from hearsay or rumor and clearly stated 570 villagers had been killed.[18]

Lieutenant Tan forwarded his version of the March 22 report to the Quang Ngai Province chief, Lieutenant Colonel Ton That Khien. In the report, Tan stated that the Viet Cong "opened up fiercely" on American ground troops, who responded with "intense firepower," thus "inflicting injuries on a number of hamlet residents because the VC mingled with the population." According to Tan, "casualties were unavoidably caused to the hamlet's residents during the firefight." Citing the long history of Viet Cong activity in the area, Tan did not personally inspect My Lai (4) or any other hamlet in Son My.[19]

Do Dinh Luyen returned some days later with more information, including a list of over four hundred names of those allegedly killed on March 16. Luyen still claimed forty-eight Viet Cong dead and fifty-two wounded, but that in retaliation for the death of the one GI, he alleged, the Americans systematically killed more than four hundred villagers. Tan then submitted a new report to Colonel Khien on April 11 that included specific allegations, including that the Americans "assembled, shot, and killed more than 400 people at Tu Cung hamlet and ninety more people in Co Luy hamlet of Son My village." While he accepted that the Viet Cong could not "be held blameless" for attacking the Americans, Tan nonetheless alleged, "The Americans in anger killed too many civilians." Tan concluded his report to Colonel Khien with an unusually strong appeal: "Really an atrocious attitude if it cannot be called an act of insane violence. Request that you intervene on behalf of the people." Tan claimed he copied the report to the MACV Quang Ngai Advisory Section, the 2nd ARVN Division headquarters, and to his American counterpart in the Son Tinh District, Major David Gavin.[20]

Throughout this period from March 16 through mid-April, Viet Cong propaganda leaflets and radio broadcasts repeatedly described the atrocities at My Lai in grim, if not accurate, detail, obviously hoping to exploit the incident. The material clearly alleged that American forces had killed elderly villagers and children and even raped and killed pregnant women. A notice titled "Concerning the Crimes Committed by US Imperialists and Their Lackeys Who Killed More Than 500 Civilians of Tinh Khe Village (Son My, Son Tinh District)" described how American soldiers destroyed homes, shot livestock, and killed noncombatants, with "blood all over," declaring, "This was by far the most barbaric killing in human history."[21] A Viet Cong broadcast, titled "The American Devils Show Their True Form," demanded revenge, urging listeners to kill as many American soldiers as possible: "HE WHO HOLDS AN AMERICAN GUN SHOULD AIM AT THE AMERICANS [*sic*] HEADS AND PULL THE TRIGGER!"[22]

Viet Cong propaganda concerning Son My continued to surface through late 1969, by which time the allegations against American troops for the events of March 16, 1968, had become public in the United States. As early as April 1968, however, interrogation of captured Viet Cong revealed that many Viet Cong wore red armbands as a symbolic reminder of their pledge to avenge the atrocities committed in Son My. Many Vietnamese and American officials dismissed these leaflets and broadcasts as exaggerated propaganda designed to humiliate the Americans and South Vietnamese in Quang Ngai Province.

In response to Lieutenant Tan's April 11 report and captured Viet Cong propaganda leaflets, Major Pham Van Pho, the head of intelligence for the 2nd ARVN Division, summarized the claims in an April 12 memo to the commander of the Division, then Colonel Nguyen Van Toan. The memo described the nature and purpose of the Viet Cong leaflets and briefly outlined the Son Tinh District chief's report, which alleged that American forces had killed at least four hundred villagers. Colonel Toan did not dismiss the claim but instead requested that the Quang Ngai Sector "review the investigation," writing in the margins of the memo, "If there is nothing to it, have the District rectify the report; If it is true, link up with the Americal Division to have this stopped." Colonel Toan also alerted the commander of South Vietnamese forces in the I Corps Tactical Zone, Lieutenant General Hoang Xuan Lam, of the report.[23]

Lieutenant Tan's April 11 letter also caught the attention of the Province Advisory Team's headquarters in Quang Ngai City. Lieutenant Colonel Guinn, Major Gavin, and Captain Angel Rodriguez, all members of the team, saw it. American advisors with the 2nd ARVN Division, specifically Major Thomas Earle and Major James Hancock, later testified to having discussed the document with Guinn in mid-April. Guinn had Rodriguez respond to the April 11 memo and discuss the allegations with Lieutenant Tan. Rodriguez submitted a one-page response on April 14 explaining that Tan had "not given much importance" to the original reports because he was "not certain of the information received and he has to depend upon the word of the village chief and other people living in the area." Somehow, Rodriguez came to dismiss charges that Tan seemed so angrily sure of in his April 11 report. Tan, too, seemed to have rethought his position and dismissed the allegations as Viet Cong propaganda.[24]

Interestingly, Guinn did not transmit any of these reports to his superiors, but he did advise Colonel Henderson and Major General Koster, both outside of his immediate command chain, of these developments. Henderson also visited Colonel Toan at ARVN 2nd Division headquarters upon receiving copies of one of the Vietnamese reports and several of the Viet Cong leaflets. Or, as Guinn testified, Henderson may have gone to see Toan after Guinn alerted him to the Vietnamese reports. Either way, Henderson took the initiative to gain control of the situation by assuring the Vietnamese that he had already looked into the allegations and found no evidence to substantiate the claims made by the village chief or the Viet Cong propaganda leaflets. Though concerned, Toan accepted Henderson's explanation at face value and considered "the matter closed."

Henderson then apparently met with Lieutenant Colonel Khien, the province chief for Quang Ngai. Again, Henderson gave assurances of his concern about the charges and offered 11th Infantry Brigade's resources to assist Khien in his investigation. According to Henderson Khien indicated that he believed the whole thing a product of Viet Cong propaganda and instead asked Henderson for assistance in mounting a campaign to counter rumors spread by the Viet Cong about Son My. Henderson then apparently forwarded copies of the Vietnamese reports to Americal Division headquarters.

In the meantime, Colonel Toan and Major General Koster had at least spoken about the allegations as early as April 12. Indeed, Koster personally visited both Toan and Khien to see if either thought the charges had merit. By April 20, Koster had requested through General Young that Henderson resubmit his oral report of March 20 in writing. Koster recalled this request as merely a record-keeping measure, while Henderson testified that Young told him as much, saying Koster "just wants some back-up here in case anything further should develop on the matter."

Henderson then wrote a two-page summary of his initial inquiry but did not include Thompson's charges. Henderson reported 128 Viet Cong killed as well as twenty noncombatants killed "during preparatory fires and the ground action by the attacking companies" and refuted Vietnamese reports that Viet Cong sniper fire had killed a GI. His interviews with Lieutenant Colonel Barker, Major Calhoun, Captain Medina, and Captain Earl Michles "revealed that at no time were any civilians gathered together and killed by US soldiers." He then cited Lieutenant Colonel Khien and Colonel Toan's view that the claims originated from Viet Cong propaganda, noting that "such allegations against US forces is a common technique of the VC propaganda machine." Henderson further recommended a "counter-propaganda campaign be waged against the VC" in the area. Henderson attached the translated script of a Viet Cong propaganda broadcast that Major Pho had originally included in his memo to Colonel Toan on April 12, and a copy of Captain Rodriguez's April 14 response, though Rodriguez's signature and name had been removed from the bottom of the document.[25] Neither Henderson nor Koster could later satisfactorily answer why or how Captain Rodriguez's signature and name had been removed from his April 14 response.

It appeared that Henderson's April 24 report would be the final say on the matter, at least from Henderson's point of view. Koster later claimed that during the first week of May he ordered a complete formal investigation. Disregarding the obvious conflict of interest, Henderson appointed Barker to lead the probe with both Young and Koster's approval. Young claimed no knowledge of Barker's inquiry or of any subsequent report from Barker. Only Henderson and Koster could later confirm such an investigation, but both claimed that it was intended to refute Viet Cong propaganda rather than establish whether American forces had committed atrocities. Henderson recalled that Barker attached approximately twenty single-paged signed statements to his report, but investigators later could find no evidence of such a report, and none of the main players of March 16 recalled Barker questioning them.

Unfortunately, Barker would never get to tell his side of the story. On June 13, Barker's helicopter collided with an observation plane over Ky Tay, near My Lai (4), killing him and Captain Earl Michles. On June 11, a South Vietnamese Regional Force (RF) unit moved in to make sure no Viet Cong occupied Hill 85 and if possible to establish an outpost atop the hill, the same one where Meadlo had lost his foot and where later in April the RF had lost six men killed in a mine explosion. Lieutenant Colonel Khien accompanied the RF into the area, hoping to finally visit My Lai (4). Major William Ford, the senior advisor for the Mobile Advisory Team in Quang Ngai, also accompanied the RF to assist with the operation.

The RF received Viet Cong sniper and light machine gun fire throughout the operation and, indeed, decided against occupying Hill 85 because of mines. The RF's approach just north of My Lai (4), however, proved accidental, as to reach the crash site of Barker's helicopter and the observation plane Ford and the RF had to pass just near My Lai (4). Viet Cong fire prevented the RF from actually entering My Lai (4), but Lieutenant Colonel Khien recalled talking on the outskirts of the hamlet with approximately twenty villagers who told him that when the firing started on March 16 many hid in bunkers while others fled to nearby hamlets. They did not see actual killing or have a sense of how many had been killed but admitted helping the Viet Cong bury over one hundred bodies the next day. Khien did not formally report these conversations.

Major Ford had no notion of Khien's ulterior motive for accompanying the RF and claimed he had no knowledge of any allegations surrounding Task Force Barker's operation in Son My, even though he had been active in the area as an advisor from the end of March through the end of 1968. Despite the "completely demolished" homes, according to Ford, My Lai (4) had become a fortified Viet Cong village complete with trenches, booby traps, and foxholes. Ford saw about twenty old men and women, and young children, but "no young men. Or young women." While he asked them about Viet Cong in the area, Ford claimed that no one mentioned anything about the alleged unnecessary killings.

Meanwhile, in May 1968, Lieutenant Colonel Holladay recommended Hugh Thompson for the Distinguished Flying Cross for landing his helicopter under fire to save the young child on March 16. Lawrence Colburn's witness statement required for the award noted that before saving the child, Thompson had landed their helicopter "between the friendly and enemy forces" to get several children out of harm's way onto another helicopter. Thompson then landed again to save the child "without hesitation or regard for Viet Cong fire." Holladay's application for the citation stated that "Viet Cong snipers had been spotted to the front of advancing friendly elements" and that Thompson had landed "between friendly and hostile forces" to remove the children then landed again to rescue the one child. A draft of the approved citation embellished the second landing with "caught in the intense crossfire" penciled in to describe the situation. The final citation, approved by Colonel Nels Parson, read:

> For heroism while participation in aerial flight as evidence by voluntary actions above and beyond the call of duty. Warrant Officer Thompson distinguished himself by exceptionally valorous actions on 16 March 1968 in the Republic of Vietnam while serving as a pilot of an observation aircraft with the 123d Aviation Battalion. On that date, Warrant Officer Thompson's aircraft was performing a reconnaissance and screening mission for friendly forces near Quang Ngai. After spotting approximately fifteen young children who were trying to hide in a bunker between Viet Cong positions and advancing friendly forces, Warrant Officer Thompson landed his helicopter near the children and moved them to a secure area. Only moments later, he located a wounded Vietnamese child, caught in the intense crossfire. Disregarding his own safety, he again landed his helicopter and evacuated the wounded child to the Quang Ngai hospital. Warrant Officer Thompson's heroic actions saved several innocent lives while his sound judgment greatly enhanced Vietnamese-American relations in the operational area. Warrant Officer Thompson's commendable display of personal heroism, unselfish concern for others, and avid devotion to duty are in keeping with the highest traditions of the military service and reflect great credit upon himself, the Americal Division, and the United States Army.[26]

Colburn and Andreotta (posthumously) received Bronze Stars for their part in what clearly qualified as a heroic action without the added embellishment of "crossfire" and "Viet Cong snipers." Thompson recommended both for the award in April 1968.[27] Thompson reluctantly accepted the Distinguished Flying Cross but later "threw it away," believing the Army "was just trying to shut me up, to buy my silence." "There were no enemy there that day," Thompson recalled, "just civilians."[28]

4 Discovery

I had prayed to God that this thing was fiction, and I knew now it was fact.
Colonel William V. Wilson, Office of the Inspector General

WHILE OFFICERS FROM THE RANK OF LIEUTENANT to major general had failed to properly investigate what happened on March 16, through half-hearted testimony and manipulation of the paper trail of incomplete reports, they could not so easily manage the rumor mill. Word gradually spread through the Americal Division and affiliated units that members of Task Force Barker had killed dozens, if not hundreds, of civilians. Rumors came from many different sources, giving credence to the wild stories about My Lai (4): that a high body count came with a low weapons count; that Viet Cong propaganda consistently claimed that large numbers of civilians had been killed by American troops; that a helicopter crew trained its guns on American ground forces; that people who knew the area claimed that there had not been enough Viet Cong in Son My to amount to 128 kills; that radio operators told of bits and pieces of radio traffic overheard on March 16; and more.[1]

Within Charlie Company itself discipline and morale deteriorated at an alarming rate after the My Lai operation. Upon Charlie Company's return to the 1st Battalion, 20th Infantry, Battalion commander Lieutenant Colonel

Edwin Beers did not recognize Charlie Company as the polished unit he had earlier handed over to Task Force Barker: "I say that the Charlie Company I got back was not the Charlie Company that landed in Vietnam in December with me." Beers found a "breakdown of leadership and communication between Medina and his platoon leaders and his noncommissioned officers" that grew worse after Medina left the unit in April 1968. Beers concluded that "they were not a top-notch outfit any longer." Even before Medina left the Company to join the 596th Intelligence Detachment in Chu Lai, enlisted men began talking back to officers and NCOs, refusing to carry equipment while out in the field, and letting their appearance slip. One sergeant, for example, alleged that his troops quit digging in for night defensive positions and that some even refused to go out on patrols. The NCOs bitterly complained to Medina, who did nothing.

Several members of Charlie Company who had been at My Lai (4) on the 16th told others what they had seen; some told what they had done. SP4 Joseph Konwinski, who served in Charlie Company but did not participate in the March 16 operation, told investigators that several members of Charlie Company, including Daniel Simone, James Dursi, and Esequiel Torres, boasted of how they had rounded up people and shot them. Even those who joined the Company after the incident bragged about what they had heard. According to Sergeant James Raynor, a combat veteran who joined Charlie Company's 3rd Platoon in April 1968, new enlisted members of Charlie Company considered themselves to be in a "good" company, "boasting" about "these people they said they killed up there" at My Lai.

Ronald Ridenhour, a young private from Arizona, had trained with several members of Charlie Company (including Dennis Conti, Michael Bernhardt, Michael Terry, Charles Gruver, and William Doherty) in Hawaii in a long-range reconnaissance patrol (LRRP) that disbanded before the deployment to Vietnam. Ridenhour instead became a door gunner in an aviation unit attached to the 11th Infantry Brigade, where he served until May 1968. He then transferred to a LRRP in Echo Company, 51st Infantry, which included Gruver, Terry, and Bernhardt as well as others he knew. The distressing and appalling stories Ridenhour heard from these men would ultimately lead him to write his congressman and others in Washington, DC, which in turn led to the Army's formal investigation of what became known as the My Lai Massacre.

Ridenhour first became aware that something disturbing had happened after running into Gruver at 11th Infantry Brigade headquarters on April 20, just before Ridenhour joined the Echo Company LRRP. He and Gruver began "shooting the breeze," catching up on their recent assignments, when Gruver suddenly asked, "Wow—Did you hear what we did at Pinkville?" Ridenhour had not. Gruver told him about seeing a soldier shoot a little boy and Herbert Carter shooting himself in the foot. Charlie Company "killed everybody in the village," Gruver told him, including women and children. A few weeks later, after returning from a patrol, Ridenhour pressed Terry, a devout Mormon from Orem, Utah, to tell him about Pinkville. Terry had been reluctant to talk to Ridenhour about March 16 but finally relented, telling the same story as Gruver, though adding that he and Doherty "finished off" several wounded civilians because "they were very obviously not going to get any medical treatment." Ridenhour thought Terry incapable of fabricating such a story and later confronted Doherty, who replied simply, "That's what happened."

In late May, Ridenhour came across Sergeant Lawrence LaCroix, who told Ridenhour of how Lieutenant William Calley and others gathered up large groups of old men, women, and children and mowed them down with their M-16s. In October at LZ Dottie, Ridenhour encountered Torres, who "laughed" about "all them people we killed at Pinkville." Ridenhour then sought out others he knew in Charlie Company to ask about Pinkville. Bernhardt, among others, confirmed what Ridenhour had heard about the 16th.

In November, Ridenhour attempted to find hard information about Pinkville from the Americal Division historian, telling the officer that he needed to see the records of Task Force Barker for an assignment on military operations for a college correspondence course. The file contained what Ridenhour later identified as the March 28 after-action report and a document that Ridenhour thought included the date March 16 and the body count of 128. When later asked why he did not formally report through channels what he had heard and found, Ridenhour told investigators he had little faith in the Army: "I wasn't altogether sure of what would happen to it if the Army got hold of it."

In late 1968, Ridenhour completed his tour and rotated out of the Army. He shared what he had heard about My Lai (4) with his family and agonized over what, if anything, he should do. Finally in February 1969, Ridenhour decided to write out all he knew about My Lai. He spent several weeks composing what was ultimately a four-page single-spaced letter that he sent via registered mail dated March 29, 1969, to over thirty officials in Washington, DC, whom Ridenhour thought might take his story seriously. Among others, his letter arrived at the offices of his congressman from Arizona, Morris Udall; Arizona senator Barry Goldwater; Secretary of Defense Melvin Laird; Minnesota senator Eugene McCarthy; Massachusetts senator Edward Kennedy; Arkansas senator William Fulbright; Chairman of the Joint Chiefs of Staff General Earle Wheeler; and President Richard Nixon. The gambit worked. Udall's office staff opened the letter, took it seriously, and took action. So, too, did the US Army. Udall's office circulated the letter to members of the House Armed Services Committee. Congressmen called the Pentagon, where Wheeler had already sent a copy to General Westmoreland, who was now serving as chief of staff of the Army after turning over command of MACV to General Creighton Abrams in June 1968.[2]

Westmoreland reacted to Ridenhour's letter with "disbelief," doubting that something "so out of character for American forces" could have actually happened. Despite the apparent "sincerity of Ridenhour's letter," Westmoreland wanted to avoid giving the allegations credibility until the Army had conducted a thorough investigation. Within days of receiving the letter, Westmoreland ordered a preliminary inquiry into the charges, a decision that set in motion a chain of discoveries and events that would grip a nation in the midst of an unpopular war, so much so that the very name My Lai would represent the infamy of the American experience in Vietnam.[3]

The Army Investigates

On April 12, 1969, Colonel Howard Whitaker, the deputy inspector general for USARV in Long Binh, received orders from Washington to look into the Ridenhour allegations. Whitaker quite naturally sought a paper trail, believing that surely the Americal Division would have investigated a mass atrocity as the one described by Ridenhour. At Americal Division headquarters in Chu Lai, Whitaker examined the daily logs of the 11th Infantry Brigade and the Division, as well as Lieutenant Colonel Frank Barker's March 28 after-action report. While Whitaker confirmed that an operation did take place in Son My on March 16, he found no charges of unwarranted killings; no evidence of any probe into such claims, despite Ridenhour's assertion that there had been one; and no mention of killings of civilians other than the twenty that the logbooks attributed to artillery and cross fire. Aside from failing to locate any record of a "2LT Kally" Whitaker did confirm that the men mentioned by Ridenhour served in Charlie Company in March 1968. None of them, however, remained in the unit, having been reassigned or discharged from the Army. Nor did anyone remain in the chain of command above Charlie Company. Major General Samuel Koster by this time had left the Americal Division to take over as superintendent at the US Military Academy at West Point. Colonel Oran Henderson had returned to Schofield Barracks in Hawaii. Lieutenant Colonel Barker and Captain Earl Michles had died in the helicopter crash in Vietnam.

In his report to the Inspector General's Office in Washington dated April 17, 1969, Whitaker concluded: "An examination of all available documents concerning the alleged incident reveals that the complainant has grossly exaggerated the military action in question. No evidence could be uncovered which would substantiate the allegations. Participants/witnesses listed in the DA Msg [Department of the Army Message] were not available for interrogation. In view of this it is recommended that USARV recommend that OTIG [Office of the Inspector General], DA, arrange to interview pertinent witnesses/participants to determine if the allegations have substance."[4]

Back in the Pentagon, Colonel William V. Wilson, a combat veteran of World War II and Green Beret, had just started a tour in the Inspector General's Office. Wilson had by chance seen the Ridenhour file and after reading the letter several times he requested assignment to the investigation. Wilson feared that "if the Pinkville incident was true, it was cold-blooded murder. I hoped to God it was false, but if it wasn't, I wanted the bastards exposed for what they'd done."[5]

At this point, Wilson had an interest only in the men of Charlie Company who had participated in the operation in My Lai (4) on March 16, 1968. Bravo Company's alleged atrocities at My Khe (4) remained unknown. He already had the names given in Ridenhour's letter, so with a stenographer, Albert F. "Smitty" Smith, Wilson set out to interview them about Pinkville. Wilson and Smith interviewed Ridenhour in Phoenix on April 29. Hoping that Ridenhour would "turn out to be crazy," Wilson instead found him "depressingly convincing." The next day, Wilson and Smith traveled to Orem, Utah, to talk with Terry, then on to Fort Carson, Colorado, to speak with LaCroix. Both confirmed the events described in Ridenhour's letter, as did Bernhardt, Doherty, and Gruver, over the course of the next several days. Bernhardt told Wilson how he "noticed, looking ahead, moving ahead, observing our American forces were gathering Vietnamese villagers in a large group and making a circle around them and killing all the people." Bernhardt said he saw at least one hundred dead, to which Wilson replied, "You saw what?" Bernhardt confirmed again, "Over one hundred dead people. Very few that I saw were of military age."[6]

Wilson then visited Hugh Thompson, now a 1st lieutenant assigned to Fort Rucker, Alabama. Thompson described to Wilson how he landed his helicopter to help people, "to get them out," and how he tried evacuating some of the women and children but that soldiers told him "the only way to help them was to finish them." As soon as Thompson lifted off, his crew saw a soldier shoot "in the pile of them." Wilson then spoke with Lawrence Colburn, who told of a captain shooting a wounded civilian, Thompson landing the helicopter to prevent American soldiers from killing a group of civilians, and seeing soldiers on the ground "killing everyone in the village." He described a ditch "full of dead and wounded people" numbering "at least a hundred."[7]

Wilson had enough damning testimony to bring Lieutenant Calley to Washington from Vietnam for an interview. On June 9, Colonel Norman Stanfield of the Inspector General's Office interviewed Calley. Initially, Calley balked when told he would be placed under oath, asking, "Can you explain a little bit more to me? I am kind of leery on what actually is going on." Upon learning that the investigation centered upon his involvement in a "war crime, to wit: wrongful destruction of a village and murder of Vietnamese civilians," Calley looked stunned: "This is kind of a kick in the deck. I don't even know what I am up against, to tell you the truth. I mean it sounds serious as hell that I am going up for a war crime." Stanfield told Calley the allegations included capital offenses under the UCMJ and that the Inspector General's Office could arrange for counsel if Calley wished. Calley replied, "I guess I better get some counsel." The interview recessed briefly so that an Army lawyer from nearby Fort Myer could join Calley in the room. When questioning resumed, Calley asked for a deal in exchange for immunity from any prosecution—he would "be willing to disclose" what happened at My Lai. Otherwise, without immunity he would answer no questions. Calley added a rambling, nearly incoherent defense of his refusal to talk: "I will have to stand, as far as the squad leaders, and everything, I would like to enforce my right to remain silent because there are just too many people involved that didn't want to be over there but did a damn good military job, to be pulled in and taken down in something like this, and probably the rest of their life to forget about. I would just like to remain silent at this time."[8] The Inspector General's Office refused to give Calley a deal. As if by some cruel joke the Army assigned Calley to a student training battalion at Fort Benning, Georgia, effective June 5. Calley could leave the Army with an honorable discharge in September if not charged before then.

On June 13 Hugh Thompson picked Calley from a lineup as the officer he confronted on the ground on March 16, 1968.[9] In July Wilson conducted a disconcerting interview with Paul Meadlo in Terre Haute, Indiana. Meadlo told Wilson how Calley "opened up and I joined in," firing clip after clip into men, women, and children.[10] For Wilson, "the case was closed. There was no doubt in my mind that a massacre had been committed at My Lai (4)."[11] Wilson interviewed thirty-six people in less than ten weeks, producing a report on July 17 that substantiated allegations of a massacre of over one hundred civilians in My Lai (4) and found evidence of attempts to cover up the killings. Wilson's report to the Inspector General's Office convinced General Westmoreland to order a comprehensive probe.

Colonel Henry Tufts and Chief Warrant Officer André Feher took over the investigation for Army CID. Feher did most of the legwork, crisscrossing the United States and visiting Vietnam to interview dozens of witnesses and potential suspects. On August 25, Feher interviewed Ronald Haeberle in Ridgeville, Ohio. If Ridenhour's letter had shocked the Army, what Haeberle revealed to Feher that day would ultimately shock the nation. Haeberle showed Feher the color slides he took on the morning of the massacre. He had been giving a slide show to civic groups in the Cleveland area since returning from Vietnam that included vivid color images of dead civilians. Feher now had compelling physical evidence that something had indeed gone wrong in My Lai (4).[12]

Feher went to Vietnam in October 1969, setting up a small headquarters for his team in Quang Ngai City. He interviewed anyone he could find, including advisory team members, Vietnamese officials, and of course dozens of Vietnamese villagers from Son My, including at least thirty-four survivors of the shootings. On November 16 he and his team visited My Lai (4) by helicopter. Villagers took Feher to the ditch where American soldiers had gunned down hundreds and to the sites of mass graves. They identified relatives in Haeberle's photographs. Some local officials, including Do Dinh Luyen and

One of Ronald Haeberle's explosive color photographs showing Vietnamese civilians recently killed by members of Charlie Company, taken during the My Lai operation, March 16, 1968. Peers Inquiry, Vol. 3, Bk. 6, P-41, Haeberle color photograph #17.

Colonel Nguyen Van Toan, continued to insist the entire incident had been the product of Viet Cong propaganda and that the dead had been Viet Cong or Viet Cong sympathizers.[13]

In late November, as Army CID continued its inquiry, Secretary of the Army Stanley R. Resor ordered a separate team to "explore the nature and scope of the original U.S. Army investigation(s) of the alleged My Lai (4) incident."[14] Both the Wilson and the ongoing CID probes had uncovered alarming failures to follow established procedures for reporting alleged war crimes in the immediate aftermath of March 16. By now, the story had become public, and questions surfaced as to the time lapse between the date of the alleged incident and Calley's arrest.

Of course, the idea of a cover-up could prove very embarrassing to the Army. Within the halls of the Pentagon, and even in the White House, some wanted to whitewash any damning evidence. General Westmoreland, however, objected and threatened to appeal personally to President Nixon to allow the investigation to continue unhindered by any political or other motives. Ever willing to take credit and protect his own reputation at the expense of others, Westmoreland claimed his threat "squelched any further pressure of a white wash," though that did not diminish White House officials' interest and concern in the developing investigation and other related cases. For Westmoreland, the My Lai revelations further tarnished his much-coveted reputation.[15]

Within the Army as well as without, the notion that the "West Point Protective Association" would shield West Point graduates who may have been involved presented a potential public relations nightmare for the Army. An Army general not associated with West Point, senior to Major General Koster, and with extensive experience in Vietnam would have to lead such an inquiry. The Army had such an officer in Lieutenant General William R. Peers, who had been commissioned through ROTC at UCLA. A stern, no-nonsense, decorated World War II combat veteran who had served in the Office of Strategic Services in Burma and China, Peers commanded the 4th Infantry Division and I Field Force in Vietnam prior to returning to Washington as chief of the Office of Reserve Components. Resor and Westmoreland hoped Peers would give the investigation credibility.

Peers began his inquiry on November 26, 1969. He and his team of investigators, which included a reluctant Colonel William Wilson, ultimately retrod much of the ground previously covered by both Wilson and Feher. Peers had decided early on that in order to explore the question of a cover-up he had to know first what had been covered up. He established a short deadline to avoid the impression that the Army "was dragging its feet," hoping to report to Resor and Westmoreland by the end of January 1970. Peers soon discovered, however, that the near overwhelming scope of the undertaking would require much more time and a much greater effort.

Peers had two other serious issues to contend with as his team began interviewing witnesses. First, the Peers Inquiry operated as exactly that—a court of inquiry. As such Peers could compel anyone still in uniform to appear before it, but he had no authority to force anyone out of service to testify. Second, the two-year statute of limitations for charging anyone still in uniform would expire on March 16, 1970. As with the rush to charge Calley before he left the Army, Peers would need to complete his report and recommend charges before the statute of limitations expired. This, of course, applied only to suspects still in service, because the Army had no jurisdiction over honorably discharged suspects.[16]

The Peers Inquiry completed its report in March 1970 after interviewing almost four hundred witnesses, including Medina, Henderson, Koster, and Calley (who refused to testify), to produce over 20,000 pages of testimony plus hundreds of directives, reports, and other pieces of evidence. Peers personally had been "stunned" by the scale of the killings and scope of the cover-up but doubted that "any of those who attempted to conceal the incident realized its full magnitude." The Army released the enormous report, which exceeded forty volumes, to the public in 1974, after the My Lai courts-martial had concluded. The Peers Inquiry's findings blighted the Army's reputation almost as much as the massacre itself.[17]

The Story Breaks

As Feher and CID conducted their investigation, the story of My Lai (4) finally broke in newspapers and on television news in the United States. On September 5, 1969, a three-paragraph press release from Fort Benning, Georgia, announced charges of murder against a Lieutenant William Calley. While the Associated Press sent the release over its wire and several newspapers across the United States, including the *New York Times*, published brief versions of the announcement in back pages, the fact that the Army had charged one of its own officers with murder "allegedly committed against civilians" back in March 1968 did not at first draw much attention. Only George Black, a reporter for the local Columbus, Georgia, *Ledger-Inquirer* made the effort to see Calley upon receiving the release, but Calley refused to discuss the charges.[18]

Rumors that a war crime trial would take place in Georgia gained some momentum and led some reporters to ask the Pentagon to confirm the story, but Pentagon officials refused comment. The story at first did not appear to be gaining any traction among the media. Even Ridenhour, whose letter had initiated the Army's investigation, at first had trouble selling his own story to the *Arizona Republic*. The Pentagon expected to be bombarded with questions about the charges against Calley, but the anticipated assault at first failed to materialize.[19]

It was thirty-two-year-old Associate Press Pentagon reporter Seymour Hersh who first made My Lai a household name in the United States, ultimately earning him a Pulitzer Prize for his reporting on the story. Hersh, who had worked as a beat reporter in Chicago and served as Eugene McCarthy's press secretary during the Minnesota senator's failed 1968 presidential campaign, first got a tip on October 22, 1969, about a trial at Fort Benning concerning an alleged massacre in Vietnam. By November 11 Hersh had his first interview with Calley. Hersh wrote the story the next day then offered it to *Life* and *Look* magazines, both of which turned him down. He turned to Dispatch News Service, which offered the story to fifty newspapers across the United States and Canada. Thirty of these papers, including the St. Louis *Post-Dispatch* and the Chicago *Sun Times*, paid the $100 fee to publish Hersh's first My Lai story on November 13. He followed the November 13 story with another on November 20, which included detailed descriptions of the killings from several members of Charlie Company, including Michael Terry, who likened the scene to a "Nazi-type thing." From this point, Seymour Hersh's name would be synonymous with reporting on My Lai.[20]

In November, reporters in Vietnam visited My Lai (4) under armed escort provided by the Americal Division. Back in Washington, Pentagon reporters peppered Westmoreland and other officials with questions about the charges. Ridenhour, Bernhardt, and Varnado Simpson consented to interviews with various media outlets. Meanwhile, Haeberle sold some of his pictures to the *Cleveland Plain Dealer*, where they appeared on November 20. That same night the CBS Evening News showed several of the photographs. Now the American public had full-color images to go along with written descriptions of the alleged atrocities at My Lai (4). Haeberle subsequently sold his photographs to the London *Sunday Times* and *Stern* magazine in West Germany, but he made his biggest sale to Time-Life, which paid almost $20,000 for the rights to the photographs. The harrowing images appeared in full color in the December 5, 1969, issue of *Life* magazine. On November 24, Mike Wallace interviewed Paul Meadlo on the CBS Evening News, where the distraught veteran openly admitted to killing women and children under Calley's orders. The interview prompted some sympathy for Meadlo, who looked just as much a victim of the war as he did a participant in the killings at My Lai (4).[21]

From December 1969, leading national magazines and newspapers gave near constant attention to My Lai not only in trying to reconstruct what actually happened but also in commenting on what My Lai said about the American war in Vietnam, the United States as a nation, and Americans as a people. Literally hundreds of stories, editorials, and interviews appeared during the first few months after the story broke. Initial informal polls of readers and viewers revealed that most Americans refused to believe the allegations. The *Cleveland Plain Dealer* received phone calls criticizing the paper for printing the photographs, including one from an incensed reader who called the paper "Anti-American." Some, including several Vietnam veterans, alleged Haeberle faked the photographs. American Legion posts took out ads supporting Calley in local newspapers, including in Columbus, Georgia, where Calley awaited trial at Fort Benning. A *New York Times* story on soldiers serving in the Quang Ngai area reported that while many GIs did not believe the stories about My Lai (4) they could see "how such a thing might have happened." One private told reporter Henry Kamm (who had visited Son My in November), "There's gotta be something missing." Another infantryman defiantly told Kamm, "The only good Dink is a dead Dink." Many soldiers believed the victims of My Lai (4) must have done something to provoke Charlie Company, otherwise why kill them?[22]

Periodicals, magazines, and journals of diverse flavors weighed in, offering both micro and macro opinions of the allegations. The *New Yorker*, for example, dramatically declared the very idea that American soldiers could have intentionally killed hundreds of noncombatants left Americans "quietly choking on the blood of innocents." The magazine further observed, "When others committed them, we look on the atrocities through the eyes of the victims. Now we find ourselves, almost against our will, looking through the eyes of the perpetrators, and the landscape seems next to unrecognizable." "To lay the responsibility on Man, or on War," the editorial warned, "is to make nobody accountable, and is to move in the direction of regarding the massacre as part of a natural, acceptable course of events." The United States could ill afford "to lighten our responsibility" by making excuses or "drawing dubious distinctions" to separate My Lai from mass killings committed by Germans and Japanese during World War II.[23]

Christianity Today echoed the *New Yorker*. Even though "the enemy's atrocities have been much worse," it argued, that "doesn't hide the appalling reality that American soldiers have been accused of gunning down helpless women and children." "Americans acted like bad guys," and the American people had to accept that "evil is not confined to the 'commies' or the 'fascists.' It lurks in the heart of every human being."[24] Similarly, *Christian Century* cautioned against excusing My Lai as a "war is hell" incident, warning, "An army of would-be defenders of freedom which is so contemptuous of the dignity of Asian peasants is likely to destroy both freedom and the people who are supposed to be freed."[25]

Contrary to *Christian Century*, the *New Republic* conceded "the hell and peril of it are that the deliberate killing of civilians, women and children among them, *is* a natural and inevitable aspect of the Vietnam war." Now "documented in blood," shooting "gooks" had become part of the American lexicon. Americans had already accepted the word *gook* as a national as well as racial term: "The Koreans were gooks, the South Vietnamese are gooks, and that is all that really needs to be said to explain Pinkville."[26]

Time told its readers that the My Lai allegations had challenged American "credibility" in the world. To regain its stature as a "great" nation, the popular weekly news magazine urged the United States to confront "its own failings," for only the nation that had "acknowledged its capacities for evil and ill-doing has any real claim to greatness."[27] The *Nation* also focused on national credibility, calling for public hearings on the charges rather than allowing the Army to investigate itself. "Nothing else will suffice," said the *Nation*, "for not only soldiers—and the Army—are on trial but the American conscience as well, and the nation and the world will be watching."[28] The *National Review*, however, questioned the sudden rash of postmortems on the "mortality of American conscience," declaring, "Irrational and irresponsible comment on Songmy has become collective madness."[29]

President Nixon addressed the allegations for the first time during a press conference on the night of December 8, 1969, focusing on the broader American objectives of the war to "keep the people from South Vietnam from having imposed upon them a government which has atrocity against civilians as one of its policies." "We cannot ever condone or use atrocities against civilians," he declared, "in order to accomplish that goal." Nixon told the reporters, "As far as this kind of activity is concerned, I believe that it is an isolated incident," trying to rechannel attention onto the positive things the United States had achieved, such as building schools, roads, churches, and pagodas, insisting that "this record of generosity, of decency, must not be allowed to be smeared and slurred because of this kind of incident." On the one hand, Nixon had an obligation to reveal to the American people the "full scope" of the incident. Yet, on the other, his administration had to be mindful of ensuring fair trials for the accused "in the midst of such widespread emotional reaction."[30]

Nevertheless, in a poll taken just after his December 8 press conference, Nixon enjoyed the approval of 81 percent of the American people. Even though 58 percent agreed with him that the United States should never have been in Vietnam in the first place, 69 percent in another poll nonetheless found antiwar protestors "harmful to public life." A later *Time*–Louis Harris poll found that the American public excused My Lai as an unfortunate part of war by a margin of 65 percent to 22 percent. A similar margin rejected the idea that My Lai proved that American involvement in Vietnam had "been morally wrong all along." Over 55 percent believed Lieutenant Calley had become the government's "scapegoat." My Lai, it seemed, simply did not bother people, or else they appeared willing to excuse the killings as the unfortunate effect of war.[31]

Congress Investigates

Members of Congress wasted little time offering their reaction to the allegations. Predictably, many hawks questioned their validity, while doves considered the incident yet another stain on American conduct of the war. Democratic senator Allen Ellender of Louisiana told the press that the villagers in My Lai (4) "got just what they deserved." Senators Peter Dominick, a Republican from Colorado, and South Carolina Democrat Ernest Hollings accused the media of sensationalizing the My Lai story and trying those charged in the newspapers rather than in a court of law. Both criticized CBS's interview of Paul Meadlo for placing Meadlo's legal right to a fair trial at risk. Hollings asked the Senate if all soldiers who made a "mistake in judgment" in combat would now "be tried as common criminals, as murderers?"[32] Democratic senator George McGovern of South Dakota declared, "What this incident has done is tear the mask off the war." The United States had "stumbled into a conflict where we not only of necessity commit horrible atrocities against the people of Vietnam, but where in a sense we brutalize our own people and our own nation . . . I think a national policy is on trial."[33]

On November 26, 1969, Secretary of the Army Resor briefed both the Senate and House Armed Services Committees on the allegations, showing them both a slide presentation of Haeberle's photographs. The images sickened Illinois Republican representative Leslie C. Arends so much that he had to leave the room. Democratic Senator Daniel Inouye, a World War II veteran representing Hawaii, told reporters afterward, "Having been in combat myself, I thought I would be hardened, but I must say I am a bit sickened," angrily adding, "It is totally inconceivable that a matter of this sort, involving over 100 people, that it could have been kept secret for over a year." Senator

Richard Schweiker, a Republican from Pennsylvania, left the briefing "convinced" a cover-up of some sort had taken place. While Resor attempted to refute suggestions that the Army had covered up the incident, Michigan representative Gerald R. Ford, the Republican leader of the House, alleged that "high Army officials" knew about the incident "shortly after it happened," but he would not reveal who these officials were when pressed by reporters.[34]

Meanwhile, the representatives calling for an inquiry found a willing leader in Democrat Mendel Rivers of South Carolina, the chair of the House Armed Services Committee's Subcommittee on Investigations. A committed hawk who doubted a massacre really occurred at My Lai (4), Rivers nevertheless convened hearings in December 1969, the timing of which further risked prejudicing the trials of Calley and others. The hearings themselves became somewhat of a farce, so much so that the initial round of hearings ceased after only three days. Hawks on the fourteen-member subcommittee literally applauded Captain Medina during his testimony and viciously attacked Hugh Thompson, who had come to Washington to tell his story. After the hearings Rivers still refused to admit a massacre might have taken place.[35]

Nevertheless, Rivers continued looking into the incident under the auspices of the "Subcommittee on the My Lai Incident," chaired by Edward Hébert, a Democrat from Louisiana. Comprising Hébert, Republican Charles Gubser of California, Alabama Republican William Dickinson, and Democrat Samuel Stratton of New York, the subcommittee conducted "classified" hearings in April, May, and June 1970 and also made a site visit to My Lai (4). Captain Medina, Colonel Henderson, Lieutenant Hugh Thompson, and General Westmoreland, among dozens of others, testified behind closed doors.

The subcommittee's report, submitted and published in July 1970, concluded that although a "tragedy of major proportions" had occurred at My Lai (4) and that the "My Lai matter was 'covered up'" in the Americal Division, the Army "overreacted" in recommending charges in "several cases." In the report, the subcommittee rebuked the Army for its supposed lack of cooperation with the subcommittee, despite the Army's delicate legal position in trying to minimize the impact of the congressional investigation on its own efforts. The subcommittee attacked Hugh Thompson for accepting "military decorations" based upon "statements which were at substantial variance with the truth." Haeberle fared no better before the subcommittee, which condemned his profiting from the My Lai photographs. Among its several recommendations the subcommittee interestingly suggested that

Section 803(a) of Title 10 of the US Code be amended to extend jurisdiction to discharged personnel who had been charged with offenses committed while in service and that no person subject to the UCMJ be allowed to "make public release" any information concerning a pending investigation or trial.[36]

The Army had legitimate concerns about the impact of the hearings on its My Lai–related inquiries and courts-martial. Secretary Resor warned Hébert of the jeopardy in which he had placed the Army by holding hearings on My Lai, cautioning that intense publicity surrounding the hearings and "premature comment on the facts of the case" threatened the right to a fair trial for all of the accused. Resor further worried that any testimony given to the committee could make successful prosecution all the more difficult by opening additional avenues of appeal. Under the Jencks Act of 1957 any statement or testimony made by a witness to an agent of the government, in this case a congressional subcommittee, must be made available to federal courts if so requested. Failure on the part of the subcommittee to make available testimony could result in mistrials of ongoing and future courts-martial.[37]

Hébert indeed defied subpoenas to provide transcripts of testimony to military courts. He further declared testimony given before the subcommittee to be classified, but in a show of compromise he ordered publication of testimony before the subcommittee to be withheld until the conclusion of all My Lai–related legal proceedings. The Army's lead prosecutor for the My Lai trials, Major William Eckhardt, later alleged that Hébert and his subcommittee "calculatingly used their considerable power to sabotage" the military judicial process. Hébert's decision to withhold testimony would indeed prove detrimental to the Army's prosecution of at least one suspect involved in the My Lai killings.[38]

Meanwhile, South Vietnamese investigators completed their inquiries and submitted reports to both the Ministry of Defense and the president of South Vietnam, Nguyen Van Thieu. From Quang Ngai Province, Colonel Ton That Khien reported to President Thieu that Task Force Barker had killed 125 Viet Cong in the Son My area on March 16, 1968. The report noted a "number of farmers" had been killed during the fighting, but officials in Quang Ngai could not "clearly" determine "whether the deaths were a result of Communists shooting," "air/artillery fire," or "the arms and ammunition of both sides." Khien dismissed "news that hundreds of people were killed" as Viet Cong propaganda.[39]

A second report from Lieutenant General Hoang Xuan Lam, commander of the South Vietnamese Army's I Corps, to the Ministry of Defense further concluded that, because "the Viet Cong intentionally brought all the corpses back to Son My to hold a propaganda ceremony to incite the people," investigators "have been unable to find evidence to substantiate reports made by the people on numbers of people killed." The report nonetheless accepted that "the majority of those killed in the incident were Communist cadre or agents."[40]

Findings

Prosecuting those involved in the killings and those suspected in the subsequent cover-up proved extremely difficult. Legal maneuvering, pressure from public scrutiny, and ignorance of military justice, as well as the simple lack of evidence, made getting a charge to trial and then obtaining a conviction a near impossible task for Army lawyers assigned to the My Lai cases. The American public seemed unwilling to pursue prosecution, as evidenced by opinion polls and thousands of letters sent by supporters of Calley and others to the Pentagon and the White House. Moreover, memories faded, for some intentionally, as witnesses became less certain about what they had seen. The Army nevertheless proceeded with its prosecutions amid public suspicion that it only wanted quickly and quietly to sweep the My Lai matter under the rug.[41]

By March 17, 1970, when the Peers Inquiry submitted its report to Secretary Resor, Army CID had charged eight members of Task Force Barker with crimes committed on March 16, 1968. In addition to charging Lieutenant Calley on September 5, 1969, with murdering 109 Vietnamese civilians, the Army charged Captain Eugene Kotouc, Sergeant Kenneth Hodges, Sergeant Esequiel Torres, and Private Max Hutson with murder on March 10, 1970. Sergeant David Mitchell was charged with assault to commit murder on October 28, 1969, and Private Gerald Smith was charged with murder and indecent assault on January 8, 1970. The Army charged now-Sergeant Charles Hutto with murder, assault, and rape on the same day. For his role in Company B's assault on Co Luy, Thomas Willingham (now a captain) received charges of unpremeditated murder of twenty Vietnamese on February 12. On March 25, the Army presented charges against Private Robert T'Souvas, Private William Doherty, and Sergeant Kenneth Schiel. On March 31, Captain Ernest Medina received charges for the murder of 175 Vietnamese civilians. The Army suspected at least nineteen others who had already rotated out of the service of crimes committed on March 16, 1968, but could not pursue prosecution of these suspects because it lacked jurisdiction.[42]

After Calley and Mitchell's trial dates had been set and the CID probe pointed to the possibility of more trials, the Army consolidated as much as possible the judicial proceedings of those charged and those who might be charged to a single location to minimize procedural delays and costs. Thus, while Calley's trial would take place at Fort Benning, in Columbus, Georgia, and Mitchell would be tried at Fort Hood, in Texas, the remaining cases would be processed at Fort McPherson, in Atlanta, Georgia.[43]

Mitchell's trial did not bode well for Army prosecutors. In a wood bungalow that served as the courtroom at Fort Hood a general court-martial tried Mitchell before a panel, or jury, of seven officers, six of whom had combat experience in Vietnam. Mitchell stood accused of assault to commit murder against no fewer than thirty Vietnamese civilians and was defended by Ossie Brown, a flamboyant civilian lawyer from Baton Rouge, Louisiana. As the court-martial began, trial judge Colonel George R. Robinson ruled that no witness who appeared before the Hébert subcommittee could testify, because Congress had refused to release transcripts of the hearings. Captain Michael Swann, the Army prosecutor, had a disaster on his hands, as he now had only three witnesses (Gregory Olsen, Dennis Conti, and Charles Sledge) against Mitchell. Many key witnesses, including Hugh Thompson and Jerry Culverhouse, could not testify, because they had appeared before the Hébert subcommittee.

Brown called twenty witnesses for the defense, many of whom questioned the integrity of Swann's three witnesses, especially Conti and Sledge. Mitchell also took the stand to tearfully deny everything. After the defense and prosecution presented their summations on November 20, the jury took less than seven hours to acquit Mitchell of all charges; the panel may have actually reached the not-guilty decision much more quickly but purportedly delayed announcing its finding under the pretense that taking a bit longer to reach a verdict would look better for the Army.[44]

The first of the Fort McPherson My Lai trials began on January 5, 1971, when Eckhardt led the prosecution of Sergeant Charles Hutto. The trial judge, Colonel Kenneth Howard, did not refuse testimony from those who had appeared before the Hébert subcommittee. Since CID and the Peers Inquiry had already interviewed most of the witnesses, Howard ruled, sufficient statements already existed that the court could make available if required. Hutto pled not guilty, even though he had previously admitted to CID that he and two other soldiers "opened up" on a group of ten to fifteen people and "was firing at the people and shooting into the houses." He had told his CID interviewer, "It was murder."[45]

Major Eckhardt read Hutto's CID statement into evidence without objection by Hutto's defense lawyer, Edward Magill, nor did Hutto take the stand to refute his CID statement. Magill instead focused on the orders Charlie Company had received from Captain Medina. Dr. Norman Reichberg, a clinical psychologist, testified that Hutto's poor, rural upbringing and his lack of basic education made it impossible for him to determine the legality of an order, an ability that a "man of ordinary sense and understanding" would be able to exercise. Reichberg told the panel that Hutto blindly followed orders and obeyed authority figures. Furthermore, despite Hutto's CID statement, none of the four witnesses for the prosecution would say that Hutto actually fired at anyone. The six officers on Hutto's court-martial panel, all with service in Vietnam, took just two hours to return a verdict of not guilty on January 14, 1971. According to Eckhardt the jury willingly ignored the Nuremberg Defense and *The Law of Land Warfare* by allowing obeying orders as a valid defense.[46]

With Mitchell and Hutto now acquitted, Eckhardt and his team of prosecutors had to reevaluate the remaining cases. The evidence against Torres, Hutson, T'Souvas, and Smith, upon reconsideration, would not stand against uncertain memories and juries unwilling, in Eckhardt's opinion, to follow the law. Due to lack of evidence, Lieutenant General Albert O. Connor, commander of Third Army and the convening authority at Fort McPherson, had already dismissed charges against Captain Willingham on June 8, 1970, Sergeant Hodges on August 19, 1970, and Sergeant Schiel on September 4, 1970. Doherty's charges were dismissed on January 21, 1971. On Eckhardt's recommendation, the next day Connor dismissed charges against Torres, Hutson, T'Souvas, and Smith "in the best interest of justice." Discharge and forbiddance from future enlistment would be the extent of their punishment for "alleged" acts committed on March 16, 1968.[47]

Only three officers, then, remained to stand trial for the killings that took place during the Son My operation. Lieutenant Calley's trial had already commenced on November 17, 1970, and remained underway as Connor made his announcement dismissing charges against Torres, Hutson, T'Souvas, and Smith. Captains Kotouc and Medina awaited trial to begin April 26 and August 16, 1971, respectively. The My Lai drama was far from over.

5 Trial

He's been crucified. Lieutenant Calley killed 100 Communists single-handed. He should get a medal. He should be promoted to general.

Mrs. Hildegard Crochet, New Orleans

THE COURT-MARTIAL OF LIEUTENANT WILLIAM CALLEY was one of the longest and most closely followed military trials in American history. Well before his trial ended in March 1971, Calley had attained a cult-like folk hero status among many Americans regardless of their stance on the war. Vietnamese survivors of My Lai probably had little idea that an American officer had been charged with murdering their neighbors and family members. The fifty-nine-seat austere courtroom in Building No. 5 at Fort Benning, complete with red carpeting, white walls, and blue drapes, served as the physical focal point for this unfolding national drama.[1]

The Calley Court-Martial Begins

Calley stood charged with six counts of premeditated murder of 109 Vietnamese civilians and faced possible execution if found guilty. He had a rather eclectic and ultimately disjointed defense team fronted by former Utah Supreme Court justice George Latimer, who had earned a solid reputation in military law from his service as a judge on the Court of Military Appeals. A veteran of both world wars, the seventy-year-old Latimer rather blindly took on Calley's case pro bono, accepting Calley's innocence without fully questioning the young lieutenant's role at My Lai. Another civilian attorney, Richard B. Kay, of Cleveland, Ohio, joined the defense team, bringing a nose for publicity but little experience with military or criminal law. The Army provided Calley with legal representation in the form of Major Kenneth A. Raby, a career officer in the Judge Advocate General's (JAG) Corps who brought experience and expertise in military case law to the defense table.

Army Captain Aubrey Daniel, a South Carolinian who had been drafted into the JAG Corps, prosecuted the case for the government. Though seasoned and energetic, Daniel had not prosecuted a case of such enormous complexity and importance as Calley's. Daniel and his assistant, Captain John Patrick Partin, immersed themselves in every detail of the massacre. They spent weeks interviewing potential witnesses and reviewing CID investigation reports and other documents, while staying clear of the press as much as possible. Richard Hammer, a journalist who daily attended the Calley proceedings, likened Daniel to a "waiting tiger," perched "on the edge of his seat," ready to pounce at any sign of weakness.[2]

Colonel Reid W. Kennedy presided over the Calley court-martial. A veteran of World War II, Kennedy had been a county attorney when, after losing reelection, he rejoined the Army during the Korean War. He had served as a staff judge advocate in Vietnam and since July 1967 as a military judge for the Army's Fifth Judicial Circuit at Fort Benning. Kennedy had a reputation for fairness, humor, and humility, all of which served the court well in the weeks to come, as he also had the difficult task of keeping the trial focused on the charges against Calley rather than a tribunal on the war in Vietnam.

In the months preceding the trial Judge Kennedy contended with numerous motions from the defense team, mostly in petitions to dismiss the charges against Calley. Latimer and his colleagues tried just about everything—pretrial publicity had prejudiced the jury; undue command influence predetermined Calley's guilt; the Army lacked jurisdiction to put Calley on trial—but Kennedy proved unbending. Only in the interest of protecting the integrity of the court did Kennedy act, such as when he prohibited witnesses and members of the court from discussing the case with the media and when he attempted to prevent further publication of Haeberle's photographs.[3]

On November 17, 1970, Kennedy opened the trial by asking Calley to answer the specifications against him. Calley firmly told the court, "I plead not guilty, sir." A jury of six officers—a colonel, four majors, and one captain—would decide Calley's guilt or innocence. All of them had seen combat; five had served in Vietnam. In his opening statement to the jury, Daniel laid out a methodical but ambitious case against Calley, which included murdering the Vietnamese monk and killing the small child as it had tried to crawl out of the ditch. Daniel described how the people of My Lai (4) had offered no resistance and stated that Charlie Company received no hostile fire as it moved through the village and yet at least seventy men, women, and children had been "executed" by "the accused and members of his platoon at his direction." After Daniel returned to his seat, Hammer overheard someone say of Calley, "God, he doesn't look like he could do all those things, does he? He looks like a little kid."[4]

Twenty witnesses testified for the prosecution, including Frank Beardslee, who told the court that he refused a Combat Infantryman Badge for taking part in the March 16 operation because they had encountered no enemy fire. Ronald Haeberle described photographing a group of villagers alive only to return moments later to find them all dead. Neither Beardslee nor Haeberle, however, had seen Calley on the morning of the 16th. Helicopter pilots and crewmembers, including Jerry Culverhouse, Dan Millians, Lawrence Colburn, and Hugh Thompson, described heaps of bodies along a trail and a ditch filled with dead and wounded men, women, and children. Thompson recounted rescuing the child and confronting American troops on the ground, but he did not point to Calley as the officer he had so angrily spoken with at the ditch. Daniel did not press him to identify Calley, later tersely telling curious reporters, "There was no reason to ask the question."[5]

At times the defense team seemed to work at cross-purposes as Latimer, Raby, and Kay cross-examined Daniel's witnesses. While Latimer tried to discredit witnesses (he attacked Haeberle, for example, for profiting from his My Lai photographs and Thompson for accepting a falsified citation) and establish that helicopter or artillery fire had killed the villagers, Raby attempted to show that several members of Charlie Company had killed villagers that day. Kay focused on establishing that the Son My area had been declared a free-fire zone and that Charlie Company had been on a search and destroy mission, thus the unit had been authorized to shoot and kill whomever it encountered. A consistent line of defense had yet to surface.[6]

Daniel waited until after the trial's Thanksgiving holiday recess to connect

Calley physically to the killings. Witnesses from Calley's own platoon, many now out of service and wearing civilian clothes and longish hair, not only placed Calley at the scene but also as an active participant in the killings. Robert Maples, for example, stated he saw Calley actually shooting people. Calley and Paul Meadlo, Maples testified, "were firing into the hole" when Calley ordered Maples to fire his machine gun into the ditch. Maples told the court he refused, thus admitting he directly disobeyed an order with no subsequent repercussions. Calley's defense team would now have a difficult time selling the jury on the idea that Calley had simply followed orders when one of his own men testified he had disobeyed a similar order from Calley.[7]

Charles Hall, Gregory Olsen, and others all testified that they saw or heard Meadlo firing into the ditch full of people with Calley standing nearby, insinuating that Calley had ordered him to do so. Some witnesses claimed Meadlo wept as he fired. Olsen vividly told the court how he clearly remembered how "some people appeared to be dead and others followed me with their eyes." Dennis Conti explained how Calley had told him and Meadlo to "take care of the people" they held along the trail, then how Calley returned a short time later to tell the two soldiers that by "take care of" he meant "kill." Conti testified that Calley and Meadlo both fired into the group of people. Latimer tried to discredit Conti's testimony by revealing to the court Conti's cooperation with CID investigators and that Conti tried to sexually assault a woman in My Lai (4) that morning, but Latimer's attack apparently took nothing away from Conti's otherwise damning testimony.[8]

On December 3, Daniel attempted to get Paul Meadlo on the stand. Meadlo had earlier refused to testify in the Mitchell trial by exercising his right against self-incrimination, even though he had admitted to his role in the killings on national television a year earlier. No longer in uniform, Meadlo nonetheless feared prosecution in a civilian, or even international, court despite the fact that Judge Kennedy had arranged immunity to protect Meadlo from any prosecution by the US government. After a thorny Article 39(a) hearing on December 3, Meadlo and his lawyer, John Kessler, exhausted Kennedy's patience in arguing why Meadlo should not take the stand—Kennedy ruled that Meadlo must testify.

Kennedy cautioned Meadlo that failure to testify would result in his arrest for contempt of court. Other than giving his name and address, Meadlo nevertheless refused to answer Daniel's questions. Kennedy gave him a second chance, which Meadlo and Kessler ignored. Kennedy had reached the end of his endurance with Meadlo, pointedly telling him, "Don't look at your lawyer, Mr. Meadlo. He's not going to help you. If anyone goes to jail, Mr. Meadlo, it's going to be you and not your lawyer." Daniel still hoped to have Meadlo testify, and before resting his case against Calley he gained Kennedy's permission to have one more day with Meadlo, along with Ronald Grzesik and Harry Stanley, both of whom had thus far eluded attempts by federal marshals to deliver subpoenas. January 11, 1971, the day the court returned from the holiday recess, was Daniel's last chance.[9]

Meanwhile Daniel still had witnesses to call. Calley's radioman, Charles Sledge, testified that Calley had ordered Meadlo to "waste" the group of civilians on the trail. Sledge also saw Calley shoot the monk and the young child—and along with Meadlo—shoot men, women, and children in the ditch. James Dursi confirmed Sledge's account of shooting the civilians at the trail junction and the ditch. Thomas Turner told the court that Calley fired multiple clips into groups of people herded into the ditch. Try as they did, Latimer, Raby, and Kay could not soften these blows to their client.[10]

Daniel rested his case on December 8, 1970, with the provision that he could call Meadlo, Grzesik, and Stanley after the holiday recess. Latimer and the defense team then took over, with Latimer offering his opening statement on December 10. Latimer set up the most anticipated day of the trial by telling the court that Calley would testify in his own defense so that the accused lieutenant could give a full account of his own "actions, conduct, and behavior." Latimer then offered explanations for Calley's role in the events of March 16, 1968, to plant the all-important seeds of doubt among the jurors. He explained that Calley had heard about Viet Cong atrocities committed against American soldiers and that Charlie Company had been bloodied during the weeks leading up to March 16 by mines and booby traps, instilling in the men of Charlie Company resentment and a desire for revenge. Latimer told the jury that the commander of Charlie Company, Captain Ernest Medina, had told his men that the 48th Viet Cong Local Force Battalion awaited them in My Lai (4) and had issued orders to kill "every living thing" in the hamlet. Calley simply and tragically followed his orders.[11]

Observers at the trial found Latimer's attempt to lay out his defense of Calley confused, if not incoherent, causing many to question Latimer's legal abilities. Some in the courtroom "sadly shook their heads" as Latimer "rambled" and "stumbled" through his obviously poorly prepared remarks, which he delivered in a low, emotionless tone. According to Richard Hammer, Latimer "had taken his opportunity and let it collapse." Latimer all but admitted that Calley had committed the acts alleged by the prosecution by allowing that Calley had not been the only killer that day and therefore acknowledging that a massacre had indeed occurred.[12]

Latimer tried to convince the court that Medina had ordered the killings. The defense team called twenty witnesses during the first week to describe Medina's briefing to the Company on March 15 and establish that Medina had told Charlie Company to kill the villagers of My Lai (4). Gene Oliver, Elmer Haywood, Charles West, L. G. Bacon, and Thomas Kinch, among others, testified that Medina had told them to destroy My Lai (4)—to "leave nothing walking, crawling, or growing" and to "kill the enemy." On the surface such testimony seemed to help Calley, but Daniel let the air out of these attempts to place blame elsewhere by refocusing the jury's attention on Calley. In his cross-examination Daniel asked if Medina specifically told them to kill women and children. Medina, they said, told them they would be facing the 48th Viet Cong Local Force Battalion and that no civilians would be in the area. Several, such as Bacon and Haywood, remembered Medina telling them to kill everything but under questioning conceded that they had in essence disobeyed Medina's orders by not killing women and children.[13]

Daniel coolly dismantled several of Latimer's witnesses and even turned some into witnesses for the prosecution by the time he finished with them. Isaiah Cowan, for example, who had served as Calley's platoon sergeant, claimed he saw only a few bodies and did not see Calley from the moment they landed until they reached the eastern edge of My Lai (4). Cowan, still in uniform, tried to deflect any criticism of his troops, as criticism of those under his command reflected upon his record as a noncommissioned officer. Daniel, however, pressed Cowan to reveal that in the past he had complained bitterly to Medina about Calley and that Medina ultimately transferred Cowan to another platoon. Although a defense witness, Cowan painted a picture for the jury of Calley as an incompetent officer who endangered his men and lost control of the operation.[14]

On December 17, 1970, Kennedy recessed the trial for the holidays. When the proceedings resumed on January 11, 1971, Daniel finally got Grzesik and Meadlo onto the stand. Grzesik proved a disappointing and uncooperative witness who gave no advantage to either side. Frequently during his testimony Grzesik said he could not remember exact details, as almost three years had passed since the event had taken place. He alluded to refusing an order from Calley to "finish them off," but Grzesik stubbornly denied knowing what Calley meant by it.[15]

Paul Meadlo, on the other hand, provided the most damning evidence against Calley. He described being "emotionally upset" as he shot down women and children, "but I still thought I was carrying out orders." Meadlo believed he had been following Medina's orders to "search and destroy" everything in the village, including "women, children, and livestock" and "took it for granted that the people were Vietcong and I still believe they're Vietcong." Calley, Meadlo explained, approached him as he watched over a group of forty people, telling him, "You know what to do with them." As he had to investigators, Meadlo repeated that he thought Calley meant simply to secure the people as the Company continued its sweep of the hamlet. Calley returned some minutes later, Meadlo explained, demanding to know, "How come they're not dead?" Meadlo replied, "I didn't know we were supposed to kill them." Calley, Meadlo testified, then said he wanted the people dead and began firing into the group with his M-16. Daniel asked Meadlo, "Where were you?" Meadlo replied, "I was beside Calley. He told me to help shoot. He burned off four or five magazines. I burned off a few, about three." Meadlo estimated that Calley ultimately reloaded his M-16 "10 to 15 times."

On the witness stand, Meadlo told Latimer, "I thought Calley was doing his duty and doing his job." Latimer coaxed out of Meadlo his belief that a soldier must follow orders to demonstrate that Meadlo did not understand the difference between an illegal and a legal order. Meadlo said Medina did not try to stop the killing, even though he had seen the results, leading Meadlo to believe "we was doing the right thing." In his redirect, Daniel relentlessly attacked the former infantryman's assumption that everyone in My Lai (4) was Viet Cong. Meadlo balked under Daniel's heated questions about shooting women and children. Ultimately, Daniel got Meadlo to say Calley, rather than Medina, had ordered him to shoot. Still, Meadlo reiterated that he "assumed everything was okay because if it wasn't I assumed he [Medina] would put a stop to it." Even at the end of his testimony, when asked by Kennedy why he had not searched the Vietnamese, Meadlo pathetically replied, "You mean the Viet Cong, sir. Maybe if we searched them they would have had a booby trap rigged up or something."[16]

With its disorganized presentation to this point in the trial, Calley's defense team now in desperation reached for something to try to save their client's life. While Calley had maintained his mental stability all along and Latimer had said he would not introduce an insanity defense, Latimer decided now to show Calley may have been somehow "impaired," perhaps even by "marijuana fumes," on the day of the massacre. Colonel Kennedy warned Latimer that any hint of questioning Calley's mental responsibility would force him to order the Army Sanity Board at Walter Reed Army Hospital to conduct a sanity examination. Calley's "internally contradictory and seemingly rudderless defense," according to scholar Michal Belknap, now "wrecked on the reef of psychiatry."[17]

Dr. Albert A. LaVerne, a psychiatrist at New York University's Bellevue Medical Center, conducted experiments with Calley during the holiday recess that included subjecting Calley to various levels of marijuana fumes to record his reaction. Latimer suggested that Calley could have "inhaled marijuana unconsciously" as he checked on his soldiers the night before the March 16 operation: a "marijuana hangover," in addition to the stress of the upcoming operation, "had affected his brain." LaVerne contended that secondhand marijuana smoke could cause paranoia, delusion, or hallucination and testified that Calley showed "minimal to moderate impairment" in his tests conducted at the Department of Toxicology at St. John's University. Nevertheless, Calley's reaction to the smoke suggested to LaVerne that Calley "was perfectly sane and knew right from wrong." Under cross-examination, LaVerne admitted he could not confirm that Calley had been exposed to marijuana smoke on the night before the March 16 operation. He did allow, however, that Calley also suffered from an unrelated "derangement" that prevented him from determining the legality of orders from Captain Medina, whom he believed Calley considered a "father figure."

Daniel asked LaVerne's assessment of Calley's personality, to which LaVerne concluded that Calley "doesn't have the characteristics or traits of a premeditated murderer. He wasn't able to formulate a judgment for premeditated murder. There is no evidence of his being a killer." If Medina ordered Calley to "kill every living thing," LaVerne contended, Calley would have compulsively obeyed the order "like an automaton, a robot." To Judge Kennedy, LaVerne and Latimer had crossed the sanity defense line by questioning Calley's ability to "adhere to the right." He quickly approved Daniel's motion to have Calley examined by a sanity board as dictated by the *Manual for Courts-Martial*. Calley underwent a series of psychiatric and physical tests at Walter Reed, all of which the lieutenant impatiently considered "unwarranted and unnecessary." The sanity board ultimately declared Calley a normal twenty-seven-year-old male who had a simple black-and-white view of the world and could discern right from wrong.[18]

On February 16, Latimer had LaVerne and Dr. David Goodrich Crane, a doctor from Indianapolis, testify to a "hypothetical statement of fact," a procedure in trial law that uses the facts of a case as commonly understood to create a hypothetical scenario from which a specialist such as a doctor or psychiatrist can, in the absence of an actual examination of the subject, offer generalizations for the court's consideration. Crane, who had not analyzed Calley, and LaVerne would use this statement to judge whether Calley could have contrived killing civilians at My Lai (4), understand the repercussions of his actions, discern a legal order, and intentionally kill another person.[19]

Crane concluded Calley had acted spontaneously and killed without premeditation. Calley "would not be capable of making a complex decision," he said. Daniel, who had spent several late nights reading all he could on psychiatry, again proceeded to dismantle a defense witness under intense questioning. Daniel got Crane to admit that he had little familiarity with recent developments in psychiatry, especially studies on stress-related conditions. Crane had no board certification, nor did he hold membership in the American Psychiatric Association. More importantly Crane had not personally interviewed Calley. How could Crane then make such conclusions about Calley's mental capacity and ability? In an intense climactic exchange between prosecutor and witness, Daniel crushed Crane: "Isn't death the consequence of an event? Was he aware of that consequence when he gave orders for people to be killed and when he killed himself?" Crane weakly admitted that Calley "was aware that pulling the trigger will kill individuals and bring about a loss of life." Daniel then delivered the final blow: "He knew the people would die? He meant for the people to die?" Crane replied simply, "Yes."[20]

LaVerne then took the stand. Latimer asked if Calley had the capacity to premeditate murder. Using the hypothetical statement of fact as a foundation, LaVerne told the court that Calley "could not possibly . . . have premeditated on March 16th in that manner, based on his lack of mental capacity on that date." Daniel then took his turn with LaVerne to ask what Calley had specifically told LaVerne about March 16. LaVerne grew flustered and asked to look at his notes, which he clumsily pulled from his briefcase. The sheets contained not LaVerne's handwritten notes but, rather, typed text of the hypothetical statement, which had been lifted from the sanity board's summary of its report on Calley. Daniel took the sheets from LaVerne and showed them to Judge Kennedy. Daniel then asked LaVerne where he obtained his information about the events of the 16th, to which LaVerne replied that much had come from the media rather than from Calley himself. LaVerne claimed he could not remember what he had asked Calley, nor did he have the questions written down to produce in court. LaVerne pleaded for Judge Kennedy's patience: "I am under stress and fatigue." Kennedy agreed, replying, "So am I" and promptly recessed court for the remainder of the day.[21]

The next morning, February 19, before the jury entered the courtroom, Kennedy announced from the bench, "It was apparent to me that Dr. LaVerne was saved by the bell, so to speak. He was hopelessly caught in what might not have been a complete falsehood at that point, but if it had been developed it would have turned out to be." With the jury present, Kennedy allowed Latimer to inform the panel that he had removed LaVerne as a witness because of a disagreement over the defense's "overall strategy" in the case. Daniel at first wanted to pursue a perjury charge against LaVerne but later dropped the issue.[22]

Amazingly, Latimer still had another doctor to call. Wilbur Hamman, a doctor at St. Elizabeth's Hospital in Washington, DC, took the stand and like LaVerne and Crane before him stated that Calley suffered from no mental illness but lacked the ability to premeditate murder. Hamman said during his examination that Calley did not use the word "kill." Instead Calley talked of "destroying" or "wasting" the "enemy," which Hamman considered significant. On cross-examination Daniel skillfully maneuvered Hamman into admitting that Calley experienced levels of stress typical of combat, then pushed Hamman on semantics. Hamman maintained that Calley had a "unique intent to kill." Daniel found the suggestion preposterous, asking, "Did he know right from wrong?" Hamman replied, "His ability to distinguish right from wrong was not affected by a mental disease." Daniel pressed further, "Could he adhere to the right?" Hamman hesitated, then replied, "No—well, to some extent, yes."[23]

Before testifying, Hamman told Richard Hammer, reporting on the trial for the *New York Times*, that he believed that individuals bore no responsibility for their actions in war. If anyone had to be blamed for My Lai, Hamman said, "I guess . . . you can only blame God." Aware of Hamman's remarks, Daniel concluded his questioning by asking Hamman, "Do you believe that no individual should be held responsible for what happened at My Lai?" Hamman replied, "It amounts to war, and if you're going to blame war on anyone, it might as well be God—you can't blame groups or individuals or nations." With no background in psychiatry, learning what he could on the fly, Daniel completely shattered Latimer's contention that Calley lacked the mental ability and capacity to commit premeditated murder. To some observers, this was Daniel's "high mark" of the trial.[24]

Calley Takes the Stand

On the afternoon of February 22, Latimer called Lieutenant William Calley to the stand to testify in his own defense, which he did for a total of nine hours over two and a half days. Latimer guided Calley through his early life and Army career up to the events at My Lai (4). Calley nervously explained how he learned in the Army to follow orders and that "nothing stands out in my mind" of his instruction on the Geneva Conventions, even claiming he did not realize he could question the legality of an order. Latimer asked Calley about going to Vietnam and the impact of the Tet Offensive on his attitudes toward the war, to which Calley replied, "It dawned on me that we weren't playing games, that we weren't supposed to be a bunch of Boy Scouts out there playing." He described the traumatic events before March 16, 1968, including the loss of his RTO and the Company's losses in the minefield. When Latimer asked what his feelings were after seeing what had happened to his fellow soldiers, Calley replied, "Anger, hate, fear, generally sick to your stomach, hurt."[25]

Latimer then had Calley describe the events of March 15 and 16. Calley claimed that Medina told them that only the 48th Viet Cong Local Force Battalion would be in the area and that all civilians would be away: "Anyone left would be considered enemies." When asked "if that meant women and children," Medina, according to Calley, replied, "that meant everything" and emphasized that "we had political clearance to destroy everything." He used the word "neutralize" at least four times in describing his understanding of the March 16 operation.[26]

As to his actions on March 16, Calley denied killing the monk but admitted that he had "butt-stroked" the elderly man with his M-16. He admitted to shooting the boy but only because he fired at a sudden movement that later he discovered had unfortunately been a small child. Calley explained that Medina radioed him to ask why his platoon had slowed down, to which Calley replied that checking out the Vietnamese had taken longer than expected. Medina, Calley claimed, "told me to hurry up, to get my people moving and get rid of the people I had there that were detaining me." Calley then encountered Meadlo and "a large—well, group of people." Meadlo told him "he knew what he was supposed to be doing with those people." Calley said he moved on, then had another radio exchange with Medina, who asked "why was I disobeying orders?" Calley again replied that the large number of people impeded his platoon's progress. Medina, Calley explained, told him to "waste the Vietnamese." Calley then returned to Meadlo, telling him that if "he couldn't move all those people, to get rid of them." Latimer asked if Calley fired at this group of people. Calley replied, "No, sir, I did not." Calley denied pushing people into the ditch but admitted to firing a few shots into the ditch, not knowing if he hit anyone. He freely admitted ordering Meadlo to "waste" the Vietnamese they encountered because "that was my order, sir. That was the order of the day," from Captain Medina. Calley, however, denied gathering large numbers of Vietnamese into a ditch and killing them and admitted to firing only about a dozen rounds that morning.[27]

Calley sat on the stand denying he had committed the very acts his defense team said he lacked the mental capacity to commit. Nevertheless Latimer pressed on, asking Calley, "Did you ever form an intent, specifically or generally, in connection with that My Lai operation to waste any Vietnamese—man, woman, or child?" Calley replied he had not, that he intended rather to "waste or destroy the enemy." "I went into the area to destroy the enemy," Calley stated emphatically. "They were enemy . . . It was a group of people that were the enemy, sir." Latimer asked "whether in your opinion you were acting rightly and according to your understanding of our directions and orders?" Calley replied, "I felt then and I still do that I acted as I was directed, and I carried out the orders that I was given, and I do not feel wrong in doing so, sir." In yet another defense swing, Latimer now refocused the blame for My Lai onto Medina. Calley added that although he did not know of an investigation at the time, he recalled Medina talking with Colonel Oran Henderson on March 18, after which he told Calley, "Well, looks like I am going to jail for twenty years."[28]

Daniel then began his four hours of cross-examination. Hammer said of Daniel, "And when at last his turn came, he almost seemed to spring with joy and relief from his chair, a caged cat suddenly freed, with his prey right there before him."[29] Daniel fired fast, short questions, expecting instant answers in return. Under Daniel's hard-hitting style, Calley slowly withered. Calley admitted that Charlie Company had not received enemy fire, incurred no casualties inflicted by enemy fire or booby traps, and had seen no signs of resistance. He doggedly clung to the notion that the people of My Lai (4) "were all the enemy, they were all to be destroyed." Daniel tried to get Calley to discriminate between men, women, and children, asking him who his men fired at when they had received no enemy fire, but Calley replied, "I don't know," a response that Calley would use repeatedly as the day wore on.[30]

Daniel had Calley describe Hugh Thompson's helicopter evacuation of several villagers, asking whether Calley considered these people "enemy." Calley finally slipped, allowing that the people had been "Vietnamese" with some children among them. He did not refer to them as he had throughout his testimony as "enemy." Daniel pounced: "There were children in this group?" Calley replied, "Yes, sir. Well, I am saying that they had to be definitely noncombatants, sir." "You were discriminating at this point between sexes?" Daniel shot back. Calley again replied, "Yes, sir." "Why were you discriminating then?" Daniel demanded. Calley replied rather incoherently, "Well, I wasn't discriminating against sexes, let me put that up. But I had a means to discriminate, and we were no longer firing on—I had been given a no-fire." Daniel later again asked Calley about the evacuation, but by then a weary Calley could not recall his earlier response, saying he could not remember if there had been women or children.[31]

Daniel then hammered Calley on the body count he reported to Medina, on why he had not recommended charges against Meadlo for disobeying orders, and if Medina had indeed ordered him to "waste" the people in the village why did he not question the legality of that order. Daniel, however, sensed Calley had nothing more to say, as the lieutenant's answers increasingly vacillated between "I don't know, sir" and "I can't remember, sir." Out of patience, Daniel abruptly asked Calley why would so many members of his platoon who had testified at his trial lie about what they had done and seen, including witnessing Calley both kill and order the killing of unresisting civilians. Calley could offer no reasons why they would all offer testimony so completely counter to his own. Daniel had enough and returned to his seat.[32]

Incredibly, Latimer kept Calley on the stand for several more minutes of redirect questions, during which he asked Calley his opinion of Medina. Calley told the jury that he considered Medina "a very fine officer, and I respected him very much. He ran a good company, and I am now and always will be very proud to have served under his command." After a brief recess, the jury asked, through Judge Kennedy, several largely redundant questions of Calley, including how he defined "civilians" in My Lai (4) that day. Calley responded, "I used the term, when I say civilians, I mean non-regular troops, civilian VC forces, sir. The VC living in the area and the VC sympathizers, meaning non-regular forces." Then Kennedy let Calley leave the stand, and the defense rested its case.[33]

Last Witnesses

As allowed in court-martial procedure, Daniel now called several rebuttal witnesses, including members of the Army Sanity Board, who declared Calley "fully capable of premeditating the murder of his victims," and other witnesses, who denied that Medina or Lieutenant Colonel Barker had ordered Charlie Company to kill men, women, and children. Louis Martin and James Bergthold testified that about a month before the My Lai operation they had seen Calley throw a man down a well and shoot him. Although Calley did not stand charged with this alleged incident, Judge Kennedy allowed the testimony because Daniel argued that it attested to Calley's capability to premeditate murder.[34]

Also in keeping with court-martial procedure, Kennedy allowed the jury to call witnesses. They presented Kennedy with a long list, which included Major General Samuel Koster, Brigadier General George Young, and Lieutenant General William Peers, among many others. Reminding the jury that their charge lay only in judging Calley and not any other aspect of the cover-up or crimes allegedly committed by others, Kennedy allowed only three witnesses from the jury list—Colonel Oran Henderson, Sergeant David Mitchell, and most significantly, Captain Ernest Medina. Although already acquitted, Mitchell invoked his right against self-incrimination and refused to testify. Henderson appeared as the last of 104 witnesses in the trial but offered little of importance and sought mainly to avoid self-incrimination, stating that he had done his diligence in investigating the allegations.[35]

Medina's testimony, however, mattered a great deal. The captain eagerly wanted to counter Calley's allegation that he had ordered the killings. The Army, however, had barred Medina from testifying for the prosecution so as not to jeopardize the government's case against him. Kennedy, however, ruled that Medina could appear as a witness for the court. Medina and his attorney, F. Lee Bailey, feared that he had been set up, as the Army had formally charged Medina with murder just the day before his scheduled testimony at the Calley trial. Potentially, Medina would have to exercise his right against self-incrimination for every question Kennedy asked of him. On March 10, however, Medina informed Kennedy he would testify without immunity. For Daniel, the development proved a great coup, since he had wanted to call Medina as a government witness in the first place.[36]

Medina testified for six hours, repeatedly denying that he had ordered Calley or anyone else to kill women and children. He claimed that at his briefing on March 15 someone had asked, "Do we kill women and children?" Medina said he replied, "No, you do not kill women and children. You must use common sense. If they have a weapon and are trying to engage you, then you can shoot back, but you must use common sense." He denied ever giving an order to Calley to "get rid" of civilians but admitted failing to report the deaths of a large number of them, an offense for which the two-year statute of limitations had by this date expired. Medina proved a solid, unflappable, and most of all, believable, witness, much more than Calley. Nevertheless, the six hours on the stand exhausted him. Medina saluted Colonel Kennedy and left the courtroom, avoiding Calley as he passed the defense table.[37]

Verdict

On March 16, Daniel and Latimer gave their summations to the court. As procedure dictated, Daniel went first, emotionally demanding the jury find Calley guilty. He reminded the jury that "a reasonable man should know without a reasonable doubt that any order if received to gather up thirty people, some children and babies, on the north-south trail and summarily execute them just can't be justified. To gather up more than seventy people and put them like cattle in an irrigation ditch and summarily execute them is illegal and the reasonable man knows it." "The obedience of a soldier to orders," Daniel continued, "is not the obedience of an automaton. When a man wears a soldier's uniform, he is still required to think, to make moral decisions, to know what is right and wrong." Daniel urged the jury to consider its obligation: "You are the conscience of the United States Army; you are the conscience of the nation." "Gentlemen," he concluded, "we have carried our burden and it now becomes your duty to return a finding of guilty on all charges."[38]

Latimer took far less time and proved far less effective in his summation.

Playing upon what Hammer noted as "old-fashioned and outdated" rhetoric, Latimer again proved not to be up to the task before him. In a "droning, often muted and inaudible monotone," Latimer warned that convicting Calley would "sear the image of the Army beyond all recognition." "Though many did things there," Latimer continued, "the indications are that this tragedy will narrow to a death race between Captain Medina and Lieutenant Calley, and I am here to prevent that from happening." Latimer alleged that those who testified against Calley had been out of service and thus did so to slander the Army. He argued Calley now played the scapegoat not only for My Lai but for the entire American experience in Vietnam. According to Latimer, where it had seemed Medina had been the target of responsibility, "all of the sudden things changed. Who becomes the pigeon? Lieutenant Calley, the lowest officer on the totem pole in this entire business." Latimer concluded, "I ask you to give honest consideration to this. It ought to make a difference between errors in judgment and criminality. I ask you to let this boy go free."[39]

After reviewing both cases, Kennedy gave the jury its operating instructions, telling the officers that they need not find Calley guilty of killing the total number specified in the counts—only one murder of the over one hundred alleged need be proven to convict Calley. The jury could find Calley guilty of premeditated murder or guilty of voluntary manslaughter if they concluded that Calley had killed in the "heat of sudden passion." With six jurors, a vote to convict required four votes, while a three-to-three vote would result in acquittal. Kennedy gave the case to the jury at 2125 hours on March 16, 1971, three years to the day after Charlie Company entered My Lai (4).[40]

They deliberated until March 28, for over seventy-nine hours in total. At 1630 hours on March 29, Kennedy had the president of the court, Colonel Clifford Ford, read the verdict. The jury found Calley guilty of murdering no fewer than twenty-two Vietnamese civilians at My Lai (4) on March 16, 1968. The twenty-two represented the jury's attempt to reconcile the variance of numbers offered in testimony. Thus, they found Calley guilty of killing "not less than one" person at the trail intersection, killing "not less than twenty" people at the ditch, and killing the old monk. The jury also returned a guilty verdict for assault with intent to murder—rather than murder—in the instance of the child. Calley accepted his verdict standing at attention before the court. After Colonel Ford read the verdict, Calley saluted "rather crookedly," then returned to his seat. Years later, a retired Colonel Kennedy maintained that the jury searched in vain for any path leading to Calley's acquittal but that the evidence clearly indicated Calley's guilt. In Kennedy's view, the jury had no choice but to "follow their oath and follow the evidence" to convict the lieutenant.[41]

The hearing for sentencing took place on March 30. Calley faced either life imprisonment or execution. Latimer told the jury that Calley, "outside of an ordinary traffic violation, was a good boy and he remained that way until he got into that Oriental area over there in Vietnam." Latimer, whose performance as Calley's lead defense counsel had been questionable, concluded by thanking the jury and offering a not-too-subtle jab at what Vietnam had done to young men like Calley: "I go away with a heavy heart for I see a life ruined." Daniel did not specifically call for Calley's execution, only "an appropriate sentence" as determined by the jury. Calley spoke unsteadily for just two minutes, telling the jurors, "If I have committed a crime, the only crime I've committed is in my judgment of values. Apparently I valued my troops' lives more than I did that of the enemy." "Yesterday, you stripped me of all my honor," Calley concluded. "Please, by your actions that you take here today, don't strip future soldiers of their honor, I beg you." Daniel could take no more and abruptly declared to the court, "You did not strip him of his honor. What he did stripped him of his honor. It is not an honor—it has never been an honor—to kill unarmed men, women, and children."[42]

On March 31, Calley again stood at attention before the court as Judge Kennedy sentenced him "to be confined at hard labor for the length of your natural life; to be dismissed from the service; to forfeit all pay and allowances." Calley saluted, then said, "I'll do my best, sir." Judge Kennedy then ordered the court "closed."[43]

Calley as Hero

Calley's conviction and life sentence caused immediate public uproar. Whether they saw Calley as a martyr for doing his duty or a victim of an immoral war, the American people overwhelmingly supported him. Public opinion polls showed resounding condemnation of both the conviction and sentence. A Gallup poll found only 11 percent agreed with the verdict and 79 percent thought the sentence too harsh. Seventy percent thought the Army had let Calley take the entire blame for the killings, while 77 percent in a Louis Harris poll believed Calley had "been singled out unfairly as a scapegoat." A White House poll reported that 78 percent of respondents disagreed with the Calley verdict and sentence. For many Americans, Calley the hero became not only a victim himself but also a symbolic victim representing all soldiers who fought in Vietnam.[44]

Sensing the public mood, politicians at all levels jumped on the "free Calley" bandwagon. Several state legislatures, including those of Texas and Arkansas, passed resolutions demanding President Nixon pardon Calley. Alabama governor George Wallace actually visited Calley at Fort Benning and took part in a "Free Calley" rally in Columbus, Georgia. Jimmy Carter, the governor of Georgia, declared "American Fighting Man's Day" across his state and urged Georgians to drive with their headlights on as a sign of support for Calley. Bumper stickers boldly demanding "Free Calley" appeared on vehicles across the country. The Veterans of Foreign Wars and the American Legion, and other groups, held rallies in support of Calley and organized telephone and letter campaigns to the White House, Pentagon, and Congress demanding Calley's release. Only a negligible minority of the tens of thousands of petitions, letters, and telegrams agreed with the verdict and sentence.[45]

A Nashville recording studio released a 45 single titled "The Battle Hymn of Lt. Calley," which became an "overnight best seller" with over 200,000 copies purchased by Calley supporters in a matter days. To the tune of the "Battle Hymn of the Republic," the song began:

> My name is William Calley. I'm a soldier of this land.
> I've tried to do my duty and to gain the upper hand.
> But they've made me out a villain, they have stamped me with a brand,
> As we go marching on . . .

The Army ultimately ordered Armed Forces Radio to stop playing the song, despite thousands of daily requests from military listeners.[46]

With his approval ratings hitting the low forties, Nixon, ever the politician, responded to clear public sentiment and ordered Calley released from the Fort Benning stockade and confined to his apartment, as he had been during his court-martial. Nixon and his advisors noticed that both hardcore hawks and peaceniks viewed Calley as a martyr. Whether they considered Calley a hero or villain, neither group believed Calley should be the scapegoat for doing his duty or the victim of an immoral war. Legally, Nixon had little room to act on Calley's behalf. Granting clemency at this early stage would undermine the entire military justice system; doing nothing offended Nixon's political instincts. Technically, Nixon could review only cases involving death sentences, but Nixon's special counsel, Chuck Colson, came up with the idea of returning Calley to his apartment until his appeal had been decided. Nixon further decided that as president of the United States he would be the final reviewer of Calley's case, once Calley's defense team had exhausted all avenues of appeal.[47]

While Nixon's decision to return Calley to his apartment appeased the American public and many in Congress, it appalled Aubrey Daniel so much that he wrote an impassioned letter to Nixon angrily protesting the president's action. Calley's trial had been "conducted in the finest tradition of our legal system," yet Daniel "was shocked and dismayed" at public reaction to the verdict and sentence. He complained to Nixon "how shocking it is if so many people across this nation have failed to see the moral issue which was involved in the trial of Lieutenant Calley—that it is unlawful for an American soldier to summarily execute unarmed and unresisting men, women, children, and babies." Nixon's intervention, Daniel wrote, had "damaged the military judicial system and lessened any respect it may have gained as a result of these proceedings." "For this nation to condone the acts of Lieutenant Calley," he continued, "is to make us no better than our enemies and make any pleas by this nation for the humane treatment of our own prisoners meaningless." For Daniel, Nixon's interference also undermined future trials: "Legal processes of this country must be kept free from any outside influences."[48]

Daniel's plea joined that of other voices in the wilderness supporting the court-martial decision. Writing in *Commonweal*, Michael Novak declared, "Those who so vigorously supported Calley—George Wallace among them—are now committed to a mass murderer." Americans could "feel sympathy" for Calley, Novak noted, but "they cannot approve of what he did."[49] A review of the reactions to the Calley verdict in *Senior Scholastic* included that of the *Los Angeles Times*, which deemed the verdict "just" and "necessary," and that of the *Courier-Journal* of Louisville, which proclaimed, "Those who did it and those who sent them to do it and those who looked the other way or refused to believe what was being done" all shared in Calley's guilt.[50] The *New York Times* agreed that Calley's "guilt was beyond question," but so long as the American people "backed away from demanding the full accounting that justice and conscience require" Calley simply remained a "scapegoat."[51] The *Washington Evening Star* thought the Calley jury had little choice in finding the lieutenant guilty, while the *Wall Street Journal* could not fathom the public's implied approval of Calley's acts. The *Chicago Tribune* also agreed with the verdict, though the paper noted the Viet Cong had also committed atrocities. Still, the *Tribune* conceded, "Two wrongs, of course, don't make a right."[52] Such voices of reason, however, held little sway with the strange bedfellows that now hailed Calley as "their" hero.

In reaction to the My Lai investigations and trials, several groups such as the Citizens Commission of Inquiry into US War Crimes in Indochina staged rallies and hearings to expose atrocities committed by American soldiers. Among these groups, Vietnam Veterans Against the War (VVAW) had become most prominent and considered most dangerous by conservative "super-patriots." Calling themselves the "Winter Soldiers," members of VVAW held hearings in February 1971 in Washington, DC, where over one hundred veterans testified, detailing atrocities they had either heard of or supposedly witnessed, to show that My Lai had not been an isolated incident or aberration. In late April, the Winter Soldiers organized a massive antiwar protest dubbed Dewey Canyon III, playing upon the Dewey Canyon I and II operations along and across the Laotian border. Veterans in crumpled, faded fatigues staged mock "invasions" of the capital and other locations in Washington, DC, while others publically tossed their decorations onto the steps of the Lincoln Memorial in angry protest. One of the leaders of VVAW, a then–relatively unknown Navy veteran named John Kerry, actually testified before the Senate Foreign Relations Committee, telling senators that the American war in Vietnam had been wrong. "We are asking Americans to think about that," Kerry told them, "because how do you ask a man to be the last man to die in Vietnam? How do you ask a man to be the last man to die for a mistake?"[53]

Calley Appeals

Reviews in accordance with the UCMJ proceeded, as did Calley's appeal of his verdict and life sentence. On August 18, 1971, Lieutenant General Albert O. Connor, the convening authority in Calley's court-martial, exercised his prerogative to affirm the jury's guilty verdict but reduce Calley's life sentence to twenty years' confinement at hard labor.

Meanwhile, Calley's lawyers pursued twin avenues of adjudication for their client. On January 27, 1972, George Latimer wrote to President Nixon to request clemency for Calley, but Nixon's lawyers advised against such action, noting that Nixon had already publically said he would review the case once all petitioners in the case had exhausted all avenues of appeal. According to provisions in the UCMJ, Calley could still petition the Army for clemency. After having made the initial request for a hearing in June 1972, Calley and Latimer finally got their day before a clemency board on November 27 that same year. Calley's petition outlined how he had been the only soldier convicted in the My Lai killings, and because of his confinement since the fall of 1969, the petition argued, Calley had served enough time, exhibiting model behavior throughout his confinement and trial. Calley asked the board to suspend his sentence with time served, but based upon its recommendation, then–secretary of the Army Robert F. Froehlke rejected Calley's petition in May 1973.

Calley's other avenue lay in formal reviews of his trial and his right to appeal the guilty verdict. As the convening authority, General Connor had already reduced Calley's life sentence to twenty years. In April 1974, new secretary of the Army, Howard "Bo" Callaway, affirmed Calley's guilty verdict but further reduced his sentence to ten years to include time served since 1969. According to sentencing rules, ten-year sentences provided for possible parole after serving one-third of the sentence. Basing his decision on the possibility that Calley believed he had followed lawful orders, Callaway cleared the way for Calley to be eligible for parole in November 1974.

Nixon now had three possible courses of action in his final review of the case. He could commute Calley's sentence even further, pardon Calley, or do nothing and let Callaway's review stand in expectation of Calley's parole. After consulting with his White House advisors, on May 3, 1974, Nixon announced that he had reviewed Calley's case and had determined to take no further action.

Calley and his lawyers also pursued every appeal process available through the Army Court of Military Review, the Court of Military Appeals, the US District Court for the Middle District of Georgia, and the US Court of Appeals for the Fifth Circuit. A complex series of appeals, petitions for a new trial, and writs of habeas corpus ultimately met rejection. In the end, even the Supreme Court refused to review Calley's case. On November 8, 1974, Secretary of the Army Callaway approved Calley's parole. On November 19, Calley walked away from confinement, and the Army, for the last time.[54]

6 Responsibility

I did not think it was any more wrong afterwards than I did at the time I saw it. Today, the more I think about it today, I find more reasons to justify it, but I don't feel that it was right.

Gregory Olsen, 1st Platoon, Charlie Company

THE END OF CALLEY'S TRIAL was not the end of the My Lai–related administrative and judicial proceedings. In March 1969, three cases remained to be tried by military courts. Nevertheless, even before these trials ended, the Army was hard at work to ensure there would be "no more Calleys."

The Medina Court-Martial Begins

Captain Ernest Medina's court-martial got under way on August 16, 1971, at Fort McPherson. Major William Eckhardt led the prosecution team, while Medina had acquired the services of prominent defense attorney F. Lee Bailey. The five-member jury included two colonels, two lieutenant colonels, and one major, all of whom had served in Vietnam. Colonel Kenneth Howard sat as trial judge. Medina faced charges of assault against the prisoner over whose head he had shot to get the prisoner to talk, the murder of the woman whom he claimed had been armed, the murder of a child, and the premeditated murder of at least one hundred Vietnamese civilians who had been killed by soldiers under his command.[1]

To convince the jury of Medina's guilt, Eckhardt focused the government's case on command responsibility, alleging in his opening remarks that Medina had direct knowledge that men under his command "were rounding up" noncombatants. In failing to intervene to stop the "carnage," Medina thus gave "protection and encouragement to his men in the perpetration of murder." *The Law of Land Warfare* held a commander responsible for war crimes committed by those under his command if he had knowledge of the act or that such an act was about to be committed and failed to take appropriate action. This definition of command responsibility came from the Yamashita Standard, which held Japanese General Tomoyuki Yamashita responsible for atrocities committed by forces under his command in the Philippines during World War II. Even though Yamashita did not order such acts, he failed to prevent them. He should have known about them but took no action when he did learn of them. A war crimes tribunal after the war found Yamashita guilty and ordered his execution. Eckhardt believed Medina should be held to the same precedent. Colonel Howard's interpretation of the standard proved very restrictive, maintaining that Medina had to have actual knowledge of the killings. Eckhardt would have to show that Medina had been present at the scene with knowledge of killing taking place or about to take place and had failed to stop it. To prove his client's innocence, Bailey told the jury that on the morning of March 16 Medina took appropriate action by ordering a cease-fire as soon as he learned of the killings. Because Medina remained on the periphery of My Lai (4) with his command group, Bailey argued, he could not have had direct knowledge of the killings as they happened.[2]

Before the trial, Medina took a lie-detector test at the request of Bailey, during which both Bailey and Eckhardt asked Medina dozens of questions. Military courts did not accept results of lie-detector tests, or polygraphs, into evidence; however, anything the subject said during the procedure could be admissible. When asked, "Did you intentionally infer to your men that they were to kill unarmed, unresisting noncombatants?" the test indicated Medina gave a truthful response—"No." As part of a peak of tension test, Medina responded to the question "Did you know that your men were killing unarmed, unresisting noncombatants?" for ninety-minute time intervals for the days of March 15 through March 17. The polygraph machine registered flat readings except for 0730–0900 hours of March 16, when Medina sent the needle "off the chart." Eckhardt believed Medina may not have intended for such killing to happen, but he certainly knew it was happening at the time it happened: "This group got out of control and he refused to stop it."[3]

On August 18, Bailey tried to get Colonel Howard to accept the polygraph results as evidence. In Bailey's opinion the results clearly proved Medina did not order the killings. This, combined with the lack of evidence that Medina had actual knowledge of the killings, for Bailey, warranted dismissing the charges altogether. Eckhardt had already accepted that Medina did not order the killings, but the tenacious prosecutor maintained Medina had actual knowledge that soldiers under his command killed noncombatants. With the jury absent from the courtroom, Howard heard seven polygraph experts, among them the chief polygraph advisor to Army CID, Robert A. Brisentine, testify on the dependability of lie-detector tests rather than to the actual results. Howard ultimately allowed Brisentine to testify only as to what Medina said to him during the polygraph test. Brisentine told the court that Medina had told the truth about not ordering mass killings of civilians and regretted his "loss of control over his men" and that Medina likely knew of individual killings early on the morning of the operation "but didn't want to believe that mass killings were being committed." By the time Medina realized killings might have been happening, "he thought it was too late to do anything."[4]

For the prosecution, Eckhardt called dozens of witnesses, but only Louis Martin, one of the radio operators now discharged from service, testified that Medina had been within ninety feet of the soldiers doing the killing. He could not say, however, whether Medina actually saw it take place. Bailey "sharply assailed" Martin's testimony, claiming that Martin's memory relied more on "assumption rather than fact" and suggested that, because of the dense vegetation and layout of My Lai (4), there could be a lot of things within that ninety feet to obstruct one's line of sight and distort sound. Robert Mauro, who had been in Lieutenant William Calley's 1st Platoon, reminded the jury of this in his testimony, telling them that the thick undergrowth around My Lai (4) "might have prevented Captain Medina from observing what his men were doing elsewhere."[5]

Medina took the stand for three hours on September 16 and denied knowing the enormity of the massacre until over a year after it had happened. He explained issuing the cease-fire order only after seeing some corpses on a trail and claimed no knowledge of the masses of bodies left in ditches by Calley and others. Medina denied Calley's allegation that he had ordered the killing of civilians, and he called Calley a "weak officer who was disliked by his men." When asked by Bailey if he intended to kill the prisoner, Medina replied, "No sir, my weapon was on safety when I pointed it squarely between his eyes. I would not have fired and killed him, sir." As for shooting the woman, Medina recalled thinking, "My God, she's got a hand grenade" as he instinctively reacted to her sudden movement, thereby portraying the incident as "justifiable battlefield homicide." Earlier in the trial Eckhardt had Hugh Thompson and Lawrence Colburn testify that they saw Medina shoot the woman, but under Bailey's cross-examination they admitted they might have reacted in the same way.[6]

Bailey requested that Calley appear and testify, a move that "startled" Eckhardt and the prosecution team. At his court-martial Calley had testified that Medina had ordered him to kill civilians, a charge that Medina denied in his testimony at the same trial. Bailey, however, believed Calley had "changed his story" and wanted him to appear as a defense witness. If Calley testified that Medina issued such an order, then the court could charge Calley with perjury. Likewise, if Calley refused to appear, the court could hold him in contempt and sentence him to an additional five years' imprisonment, as he remained under the jurisdiction of the UCMJ. Colonel Howard declared he would not force Calley to answer self-incriminating questions. Bailey then withdrew his request, telling reporters afterward, "There is no need to parade him here."[7]

As for the charge of the child's murder, Colonel Howard dropped it after Gene Oliver, now out of service and thus free from prosecution, came forward and testified that he, rather than Medina, had shot the boy. Oliver described how he had instinctively shot at a movement, which turned out to be the boy. No one, Oliver said, ordered him to shoot. Medina claimed he may have yelled, "Shoot!" then quickly shouted, "Don't shoot!" upon seeing the boy, but the countermand came too late. Eckhardt recalled Oliver to the stand and accused him of making threatening statements against him and his assistant prosecutor, Captain Franklin Wurtzel. Oliver denied it, but Bailey nevertheless demanded a mistrial because Eckhardt had accused Oliver in front of the jury. Colonel Howard refused to grant one.[8]

Michael Bernhardt may have been Eckhardt's biggest disappointment. The day before his testimony on August 25, Bernhardt told Medina's two military lawyers, Captains Mark Kadish and John R. Truman (from Independence, Missouri, and a grandnephew of former president Harry Truman), that he would deliberately not tell the truth on the stand. Kadish and Truman told Bailey. When Bernhardt took the stand Bailey immediately asked for a hearing without the jury in the courtroom to discredit Bernhardt as a prosecution witness. Bailey asked him, "Would you lie if you thought it would serve the ends of justice?" Bernhardt replied, "Okay, in answer to your question, yes, I would." Eckhardt had to withdraw him as a prosecution witness.

To add to what had already been a bad day for the prosecution, Eckhardt then called Frederick Widmer to the stand. Despite being out of service and not subject to prosecution, Widmer promptly "invoked the constitutional privilege against self-incrimination and declined to testify." Colonel Howard cited Widmer for contempt, but Widmer appealed the citation and did not testify further in the Medina trial.[9]

Bailey then called Captain Robert Hicks to testify before Judge Howard that Calley had told him that Medina had been "certainly surprised" when Calley informed Medina of the mass killings during the day on March 16, 1968. (The jury members had been removed from the courtroom because Howard had to decide if Hicks's testimony would be admitted as evidence.) Eckhardt objected to Hicks's claim as hearsay.[10] The next day Howard nonetheless allowed Hicks's testimony into the record. Howard also allowed testimony from a lie-detector expert Bailey had called to the stand to impeach the earlier testimony of Louis Martin, who claimed Medina had been nearby and therefore must have had knowledge of the killings. After testifying Martin apparently told the defense team that he now doubted what he had said on the stand but he did not want to reappear in court. Bailey convinced him to take a polygraph test in return for not putting him back on the stand. Before taking it Martin told the expert that he had suffered from "illusions and delusions" much of his life and "was no longer sure the group of victims had really existed." Eckhardt lost yet another round.[11]

None of the fifty other witnesses would say that Medina had been in the actual presence of any killing or that Medina had ordered anyone specifically to kill civilians. All praised Medina as an effective and fair commander. On September 17, Judge Howard reduced the charge of killing no fewer than one hundred civilians from premeditated murder to involuntary manslaughter, the conviction of which carried a maximum sentence of three years. For Eckhardt and his prosecution team, nothing went right. Mary McCarthy, a reporter covering the Medina trial, heard a fellow journalist whisper after the Bernhardt fiasco, "I get the feeling somebody is betraying Eckhardt." Either that, or, as McCarthy later suggested, Bailey had simply outmatched and outwitted the prosecution.[12]

On September 22, 1971, Bailey and Eckhardt offered their closing arguments to the jury, which then retired to consider the fate of Captain Ernest Medina. They returned quickly after less than an hour of deliberation to announce acquittal on all charges. A "stifled cheer and some handclapping" greeted the verdict. Medina embraced his wife then told reporters outside the courtroom that during the trial he never lost "faith in military justice." During and after the trial observers speculated on the prosecution's level of preparation and suggested further that the Army had stacked the trial against conviction by placing so many southerners on the panel and having a southerner, Howard, judge the trial. Southerners, the theory went, tended to be pro-war, pro-military, and more forgiving of mass violence. Others, like Mary McCarthy, dismissed such conspiracies and suggested that the case against Medina simply had no merit. At best, the jury could have convicted Medina of dereliction of duty, but since that charge had expired, the Army had little choice but to proceed with ultimately fruitless charges.[13]

Before Medina's trial, Captain Eugene Kotouc's court-martial for assault and deliberate maiming of a prisoner had also taken place at Fort McPherson. Defended by former Republican governor of Nebraska Robert C. Crosby, Kotouc contended that cutting off the prisoner's finger had been an accident—the knife had simply "slipped" as he tried to frighten the prisoner. Trial judge Colonel Madison Wright instructed the jury to find Kotouc not guilty of assault. Wright reminded the jury of seven officers that interrogation procedures in place in 1968 would have led Kotouc to believe he could threaten the prisoner with violence in order to obtain information. Of the seven witnesses called by Major Eckhardt against Kotouc, only Frederick Widmer could positively identify Kotouc as the captain who had committed the act against the Viet Cong prisoner. To convict on the charge of deliberately maiming the prisoner in violation of Article 124 of the UCMJ, the jury had to be certain that Kotouc had acted with the intent to injure. On April 29, 1971, after only three days of trial and less than one hour of deliberation, the jury returned a verdict of not guilty.[14]

Charges from Peers

The Peers Inquiry accused thirty individuals of having knowledge of the killings, making false reports, suppressing information, false swearing, failing to report a felony, and committing similar derelictions of duty. Of the thirty, four were deceased—Lieutenant Colonel Frank Barker, Captain Earl Michles, Second Lieutenant Stephen Brooks, and Second Lieutenant Michael Lewis. Seven had left the Army and returned to civilian life and thus could not be prosecuted, leaving nineteen active-duty officers who could be charged in the cover-up, including Major General Samuel Koster and Colonel Oran Henderson. Of the fourteen the Army continued to investigate, only Colonel Henderson actually went to trial to answer charges surrounding the cover-up. The remainder either suffered administrative punishments, which, contrary to popular perception, carried some deterrent weight in the military, or had charges dropped for lack of evidence.[15]

As commanding general of the First Army at Fort Meade, Lieutenant General Jonathan O. Seaman, a West Point graduate who had commanded a division in Vietnam and now approached retirement, served as the convening authority for the charges stemming from the Peers Inquiry. Though the Article 32 investigation on Koster had been complete for over three months, Seaman waited until the day before his retirement to dismiss charges against Koster "in the interest of justice." Seaman, however, did give Koster a severe letter of censure in which he held Koster "personally responsible" for failing to follow established procedures and submit required reports on the incident. The Army, with Westmoreland's approval, subsequently demoted Koster to brigadier general, placed an additional letter of censure in his personnel file, and revoked his Distinguished Service Medal, which had been awarded by Westmoreland.[16]

Seaman approved the court-martial of only one case, that of Colonel Henderson, whose court-martial would be the final My Lai trial. As recommended by the Peers Inquiry, the Army accused Henderson of dereliction of duty for not reporting and properly investigating a possible war crime as well as for giving false testimony. If guilty, he faced up to six years in prison and dismissal from service. The trial jury of two generals and five colonels sat to hear opening arguments on August 5, 1971. Army Major Carroll J. Tichenor hoped to prove Henderson guilty of "neglect and willful deceit" in his involvement in the My Lai cover-up, while Henderson's defense lawyer, New

York attorney Henry B. Rothblatt, intended to show that his client had done due diligence in his investigation during March 1968. Held at Fort Meade in Maryland, the trial was presided over by Colonel Peter S. Wondolowski, an experienced military judge.[17]

Tichenor opened his case against Henderson on August 23. In all, he would call sixty-two witnesses in an attempt to show that Henderson had failed to investigate properly the killing of civilians at My Lai (4), to uncover the massacre, and to report the allegations to his superiors. Among these witnesses, Jay Buchanan testified that Henderson had collectively asked them about their conduct during the operation upon returning to LZ Dottie on March 18, with no signed statements or no one taking an oath, which allowed Tichenor to show that Henderson had not conducted a proper investigation. Major Charles Calhoun testified that Henderson had not questioned him about any "misconduct" of Charlie Company. Now–Brigadier General Koster testified that he had taken Henderson's report at "face value," thus confirming his own negligence. Hugh Thompson testified but did not identify Henderson as the colonel whom he had spoken with on March 18, as he had done before the Peers Inquiry. Jerry Culverhouse and Lawrence Colburn also refused to identify Henderson, as they too had both done before the inquiry. Because of this, Judge Wondolowski dismissed the charge against Henderson for lying to Peers.[18]

Tichenor also called Frederic Watke (now a lieutenant colonel), who told the jury how he had reported "unnecessary killing" alleged by his helicopter crews to Lieutenant Colonels Frank Barker and John Holladay and how he had told Henderson of the massacre on March 18 in the presence of Brigadier General George Young, Barker, and Holladay. Holladay confirmed Watke's version of events in his testimony. Colonel William Wilson testified, as did Lieutenant General William Peers, both claiming Henderson admitted to them that on March 16, 1968, he knew that soldiers from Task Force Barker had killed dozens of women and children.

Rothblatt called Young to the stand for the defense. Young claimed he knew nothing about large numbers of civilians being killed on March 16 and had told Henderson to investigate only Thompson's allegation that he had prevented soldiers from firing upon some unarmed civilians whom Young had understood to have been caught in a cross fire. Rothblatt also called Medina, who shocked the court by admitting on the stand that in March 1968 he lied to Henderson about the number of civilians killed. Medina further revealed that he knew at the time that men under his command had killed dozens of men, women, and children. Having just resigned from the Army and now out of uniform, Medina escaped perjury charges. Medina said he lied because of possible "repercussions involving the United States and other nations" and that he "was concerned about my family and my role as a father." Tichenor asked Medina, "Do you realize you have completely disgraced and dishonored the uniform you wore?" Medina solemnly responded "Yes, sir."[19]

Henderson testified last, maintaining that he had believed his subordinates' reports that no massacre had taken place and that he had no personal knowledge of any civilian deaths beyond the twenty that Medina had indicated. Henderson further claimed that Young had only told him to "inquire" about Thompson's story and nothing more. Henderson believed Medina and had no reason to doubt Barker's April 24 report to Koster.

On December 16, 1971, Colonel Wondolowski issued his instructions to the court-martial jury. He reminded its members that Henderson did not stand accused of any direct involvement in the massacre: "The accused has not been charged with, and the prosecution is in no way suggesting, that the accused had any responsibility for ordering, knowing, permitting, condoning, or failing to prevent, any of these crimes." To find Henderson innocent of dereliction, the jury had to be convinced that Henderson "made an honest and reasonably diligent effort to perform his duties." Wondolowski allowed that the panel could find Henderson guilty of the lesser offense of "negligence" in failing to "measure up to an objective criterion of successful performance" if they were convinced Henderson had acted without "bad purpose or an evil motive." He also instructed the jury to consider Henderson's "good character" and reputation as an officer. The jury returned after four hours on December 17 to find Henderson not guilty of all charges. While disappointed, Tichenor told reporters, "It was an extremely fair trial. I have no qualms with the result." Henderson told the press that the verdict "reaffirms the confidence any Army man can have in the military system. I feel sort of ridiculous now. The Government spent $10 million to convict me and they don't get a conviction."[20]

Ultimately, in the Army's view, only a fraction of the charges recommended by the Peers Inquiry merited further investigation, much less prosecution. As for the trials themselves, the Army prosecution teams suffered from witnesses with faulty memories (both intentional and sincere), a peculiar range of legal maneuverings and rulings, and, according to some observers, simple inexperience, all of which hampered successful prosecution of the My Lai defendants.[21]

Even Westmoreland did not escape investigation. Sergeant Esequiel Torres, who at the time still faced murder charges in the My Lai incident, brought charges of dereliction of duty against Westmoreland in September 1970. Torres alleged Westmoreland, in accordance with the Yamashita Standard, failed to prevent the killings at My Lai. The charge was ludicrous, but it was Torres's right to bring it. Despite its absurdity, the Army did its due diligence and had its general counsel, Robert Jordan, investigate the charge. Jordan advised Secretary of the Army Resor that Westmoreland had no knowledge of My Lai until receiving Ridenhour's letter in 1969. Resor put the matter to rest in an October memorandum that cleared Westmoreland of any connection with My Lai and the subsequent cover-up. Yamashita would not reach Westmoreland.[22]

No More My Lais, No More Calleys

As an institution very nearly ruined by its experience in Vietnam and in the midst of transforming to an all-volunteer force, the Army had many lessons to learn and much damage to repair. Typical of an organization in crisis, the Army's reaction to My Lai and Vietnam tended to be doctrinaire while attempting to be prescriptive. Everything from enlisted and officer recruiting and training, to combat rotation policies, to investigation procedures came under intense scrutiny in the years following Vietnam.

Concerning the laws of war, the Army concluded that it had adequate guidelines and directives but had failed in instruction and indoctrination. The Peers Inquiry listed poor training in the laws of war among the causes of the My Lai killings while an Army study revealed that during the first half of 1969 almost half of its soldiers did not receive mandatory training on the Hague and Geneva Conventions. Remedies included requiring a team consisting of a judge advocate and a combat-experienced officer to give formal instruction to soldiers on the laws of war to include, among other things, a greater emphasis on "acts of violence against and inhumane treatment of personnel; legality of orders; rules of engagement; and war crimes reporting procedures." The Army apparently thought it could achieve this by increasing the mandatory annual training requirement from one hour to two hours and having each individual soldier initial "the appropriate personnel record certifying the date of the formal instruction last completed."

In Vietnam MACV issued a flurry of updated directives on reporting and investigating atrocities, and the Army also revised and reissued various directives concerning war crimes. Army CID now had to certify anyone investigating alleged war crimes and prohibited anyone in the chain of command of a suspected individual or unit from conducting such an investigation. For the long term, the Department of Defense "Law of War" program, instituted in 1974 in direct response to the findings of the Peers Inquiry, laid the foundation ultimately for putting judge advocates in the operational planning process, and even in combat operations, to advise on rules of engagement and other matters. This new "operational law" was born in part out of My Lai, having its combat debut in 1983 in Operation Urgent Fury in Grenada.[23]

What the inquiry called "personnel turbulence" also became a common theme not only as a contributing cause to the My Lai killings but also to the lack of combat readiness of American forces across Vietnam. Though the Peers Inquiry did not recommend specific changes to the rotation policy used by the Army in Vietnam, it did suggest the Army undertake a "thorough review . . . to determine if the impact of these, or similar programs, on combat readiness can be reduced in the future." While understandably popular among many soldiers, the one-year rotation system created chaos on both the training ground and battlefield. Soldiers came and went, often in the middle of a training exercise, or worse yet, in the field, where orientation programs often fell by the wayside.

For officers the rotation policy caused even more harm. In six months, just when a lieutenant or captain gained important experience, the Army reassigned the officer to another job, usually a staff position, leaving ripened experience to rot on the vine. Moreover, the rapid buildup to meet force requirements in Vietnam accelerated normal promotion rates. In 1965, promotion from first lieutenant to captain normally took five years; by 1969, a first lieutenant could be promoted to captain in one to two years. By no means unique to the Vietnam War, accelerated promotion rates during wartime are a common side effect of wartime personnel needs, but in Vietnam the quick promotion pace combined with the one-year rotation policy exacerbated inexperience and discontinuity. "Ticket punching" by career officers to get command and combat experience on their personnel records also contributed to the problem. In the end, the rotation policy robbed all of the services of experience and long-term unit cohesion.

In the 1970s, criticizing junior officers for the American failure in Vietnam became fashionable, despite the lack of hard data to support such claims. The fact that the Army commissioned Lieutenant William Calley through its own officer candidate school seemed enough to condemn both the process and all of the junior officers it produced, allowing critics to argue that the demand in quantity diminished the quality of second lieutenants over the course of the war. Guenter Lewy, in his otherwise remarkable study of the American experience in Vietnam, blamed the deterioration of troop discipline and atrocities committed by American soldiers on a substandard cadre of junior officers. In a scathing article in the *Armed Forces Journal*, Robert D. Heinl noted that Calley had not been an aberration, as the officer-commissioning process had allowed countless Calleys to command platoons in Vietnam. In *Crisis in Command: Mismanagement in the Army*, Richard A. Gabriel and Paul L. Savage pointed to careerism across the officer ranks as a contributing cause of the American failure in Vietnam, arguing as well that Calley's actions at My Lai provided proof plenty of the degraded quality of junior officers. Even General Westmoreland in his memoir found blame among junior officers, claiming that draft deferments had prevented the Army from "drawing upon the intellectual segment of society" for junior grade officers; otherwise, "Calley probably never would have been an officer."[24]

Historians have more recently countered these criticisms of junior officers, arguing against the idea that Calley represented the lot of platoon leaders in Vietnam. Historian Ronald Spector concluded that the United States had sent the best-educated officer corps in its history to fight in Vietnam. Peter Kindsvatter praised junior officers, who in his estimation did their best in a war so very different from World War II. Historian Ron Milam's detailed study of junior officer training and performance throughout the war found little evidence to support the idea that the Army lowered standards and scraped the bottom of the social barrel to meet its officer needs. On the contrary, Milam argued, junior officers "performed their duties with efficiency and aplomb" and that My Lai made it easy for critics to blanket lieutenants with the failure in Vietnam. For Milam, the "evidence shows there was not a 'thousand Calleys'—there was only one."[25]

Largely because of My Lai the military law community reexamined military justice regulations and procedures involving war crimes–related charges. Though prohibited by the UCMJ, command influence continued to be a problem, one that heightened public sensitivities toward military justice. The lack of jurisdiction over discharged service members who allegedly committed crimes while in service also attracted comment, leading to legislative efforts to extend jurisdiction over such individuals and allowing federal courts to conduct war crimes trials.[26]

Of the more provocative discussions during and after the My Lai trials, the concept of command responsibility came under intense scrutiny. Telford Taylor, a law professor at Columbia University who had been a prosecutor in the Nuremberg trials following World War II, maintained that the United States should hold to the standards it and the Allies set in the postwar trials in Europe and Japan. These standards, namely, that following orders does not constitute a valid defense and that commanders are responsible for the actions of their subordinates, would not only convict Calley, Medina, Henderson, and Koster, but theoretically also General Westmoreland (as Torres alleged), Secretaries of Defense Robert McNamara and Clark Clifford, and Presidents Johnson and Nixon.[27] Waldemar A. Solf, chief of the International Affairs Division in the Army Judge Advocate General's Office, disagreed, citing directives, policies, and procedures already in place to prevent and report atrocities. Unlike war crimes committed under the direction of the German and Japanese governments during World War II, My Lai and any other atrocity committed by American troops during the Vietnam War could not be upheld as state policy. The United States already had appropriate standards in place for command responsibility and using obeying orders as a defense; the problem lay in enforcement and in leadership.[28]

Epilogue

For both perpetrator and victim several factors influence the memory of My Lai. Historian Kendrick Oliver contends that for Americans the memory of My Lai is now "muted," making the entire episode as a pivotal historic moment "unclear." In the American collective memory, Oliver suggests, soldiers who served in Vietnam have replaced the villagers of My Lai as the victims. Once sent to fight an unjust war using immoral tactics and brutal weapons, then returning to an ungrateful nation that ostracized them as "baby killers," veterans of Vietnam later enjoyed increased benefits from a government and nation that sought forgiveness for "victimizing" the men and women who served in Southeast Asia. The overdue rehabilitation of the Vietnam-era veteran has been nothing short of remarkable, so much so that, where once some veterans went to great lengths to hide their service, more recently some have lied to create or enhance their attachment to Vietnam. To remind the nation that a very small minority of these veterans committed atrocities risks negative, if not damaging, backlash, as evidenced by the so-called swift boat controversy surrounding John Kerry's 2004 presidential campaign.[1]

As for the Vietnamese survivors of March 16, 1968, they have been largely absent from the American memory of Vietnam. Initially, historians and commentators gave much more space to the American investigations and trials and to the Americans involved than to the Vietnamese victims. While it is quite natural for a people to focus on its own experience rather than that of the other, to approach a collective understanding, the experience of the other must be examined. For decades the true victims of My Lai appeared as a total number of killed, 504 usually, rather than as individuals with unique stories or as a collective with a common experience. No survivor of My Lai testified in person at any of the trials. Only recently, through the work of historians such as Kendrick Oliver and Christian Appy, have the victims of My Lai and, indeed more broadly, the war experience of the Vietnamese moved closer to the forefront of the American experience in Vietnam.[2]

The Vietnamese, too, struggle with a collective memory of My Lai. Many Vietnamese rely upon tradition and ritual to remember their dead ancestors and maintain a connection to their past, as practiced for centuries. After 1975, the Vietnamese government allowed only superficial and propagandized commemoration of atrocities committed by American or South Vietnamese soldiers, notably at the Ho Chi Minh City War Remnants Museum, formally known as the American War Crimes Museum. Encouraging real discussion of atrocities risked, for example, dredging up memories of the mass killings committed by Viet Cong forces at Hue during the 1968 Tet Offensive. Moreover, with a majority of Vietnamese born after 1975, fewer have real memory of My Lai and the war. Those who do remember are now part of a passing generation, an inevitable fact that permanently alters memory.[3]

This attitude changed, somewhat, in the 1990s, when the Vietnamese government first opened My Lai as a destination for Western tourists. Before, the Vietnamese government did not encourage this sort of tourism, and only dignitaries—mostly from other communist countries—few Vietnamese, and fewer Americans visited the My Lai site. Though still difficult to get to and nowhere near as developed as other parts of Vietnam, My Lai is now a tourist destination as well as a very public location for foreign philanthropic endeavors—even for Americans.

Various memorials and markers dot the now-serene location where My Lai once stood, highlighted by what Oliver described on his visit to the site as a large "socialist realist sculpture . . . depicting a woman with one arm raised in defiance, the other clasping a dead child, with four wounded figures collapsed at her feet." A small museum welcomes visitors, and My Lai survivors occasionally lead guided tours. Part of the village has been recreated, complete with a burned out hootch and dead livestock. The museum includes a display of life-sized figures of American soldiers shooting terrified Vietnamese. Tourist coaches from Hanoi, Da Nang, Ho Chi Minh City, and other locations make regular, but usually brief, stops in the area. Despite the fact that the My Lai memorial and museum appear frequently in Western travel guides, the place is rarely mentioned in similar guides published in Vietnam. As an indicator of changing times, the My Khe Resort (opened in 2005) sits along the beach near where members of Company B allegedly shot several fleeing civilians.[4]

Several philanthropic and charitable groups have undertaken construction projects and other activities, as if to make up somehow for the tragedy of decades ago. In the 1990s, for example, an organization from Wisconsin called Madison Quakers, led by Vietnam veteran Mike Boehm, established a clinic and school near My Lai. On March 16, 1998, the group, in cooperation with the Quang Ngai Province Women's Organization, began work on the My Lai Peace Park, near the My Lai site. Hugh Thompson and Lawrence Colburn attended the groundbreaking ceremony, which was reported by CBS's Mike Wallace and *60 Minutes*. It was a poignant moment in the ongoing process of healing still-open wounds from thirty years before. Still, the question begs—how much of this is about healing and memory, and how much is about the almighty dollar?[5]

Other than VVAW and similar organizations, many believed, or wanted to believe, that My Lai had been an aberration. This view held until more recently, when historians and journalists gained access to newly declassified records, mainly those of the Vietnam War Crimes Working Group. These records revealed that the Pentagon had investigated over three hundred alleged atrocities committed by American military personnel in Vietnam. These charges ranged from individual acts of assault and murder to massacres, though none anywhere near approaching the scale of My Lai. The records also indicated hundreds of additional but unsubstantiated allegations. Of the investigated claims, only a fraction resulted in courts-martial, with fewer still gaining convictions. The records nevertheless gave some credence to testimony by the Winter Soldiers and others during the war and revealed to the public for the first time such alleged atrocities as those committed in 1967 by members of a small special operations force from the 1st Battalion, 327th Infantry, in the 11th Brigade of the famous 101st Airborne Division. Several members of this highly decorated unit, known as Tiger Force, purportedly tortured and executed prisoners, routinely killed noncombatants, and mutilated corpses.[6]

My Lai, however, remains the face of atrocities, alleged and proven, committed by American forces in Vietnam. Why Calley and members of Task Force Barker did what they did on March 16, 1968, will likely never be fully understood. Several factors contributed to the tragedy: negligently vague orders; a gross lack of leadership; a toxic atmosphere of outrage and revenge over lost comrades; lax and inaccurate intelligence; inadequate training; inconsistent enforcement of directives; careerism; a flawed counterinsurgency strategy; indiscriminate search and destroy tactics; an enemy that was misunderstood and difficult to identify; racial indifference toward Vietnamese; a skewed belief that body counts measured progress; and, undoubtedly, personalities that allowed their own internal moral compasses to swing wildly. An unwillingness to take responsibility, too, played a role, a dangerous one that continues to haunt the American conscience.

While some of these factors may have been more important than others, no single thing caused My Lai, just as no single thing caused the more recent atrocities committed by American military personnel in the Middle East. In the recent Iraq War, for example, American Marines and soldiers have been implicated in unauthorized killings of civilians at Haditha and Mahmudiyah, respectively, in addition to the abuses committed by American soldiers in Abu Ghraib prison. Six service members were convicted and sentenced in the Mahmudiyah incident, while none were found guilty of wrongdoing at Haditha. Eleven soldiers were found guilty of Iraqi prisoner abuses, including the death of at least one prisoner, at Abu Ghraib. In the Haditha and Abu Ghraib incidents, officers were reprimanded for failing to report and properly investigate possible war crimes. Interestingly, journalist Seymour Hersh, who broke the My Lai story in 1969, was at the forefront of the Abu Ghraib story, writing several articles about the incident in the *New Yorker*. Similar allegations have surfaced in Afghanistan.[7] As Major General George S. Prugh, the Army judge advocate general from 1971 to 1975, grimly noted in the official history of Army legal activities in Vietnam, "No absolute insurance can be obtained that there will never be gross criminal aberrations such as My Lai."[8] Prugh, unfortunately, was right.

After Calley's trial, journalist Richard Hammer observed, "Vietnam and My Lai have ended America's innocence, ended it perhaps for good."[9] When

Ronald Haeberle's haunting photograph of Vietnamese women and children in the midst of the killing at My Lai, March 16, 1968. Peers Inquiry, Vol. 3, Bk. 6, P-40, Haeberle color photograph #18A.

looking at Ronald Haeberle's horrifying photograph of seven women and girls huddled in indescribable fear, one is looking simultaneously at lost innocence and imminent death, much in the same way as in images of the Holocaust. As horrifying as this and Haeberle's other photographs appear, they are the most graphic physical reminder that Americans killed hundreds of villagers at Son My, making deniability and false memory difficult. Historian and teacher Claude Cookman, who served in Vietnam in 1968, urges students to study these photographs not as an admission of "collective guilt" but rather "to acknowledge the moral ambiguity inherent in all wars and accept the evil our country has perpetrated along with the good."[10] To forget an event like My Lai by either accepting that atrocities are part of war or creating a false memory that belittles or denies such incidents risks the irreparable erosion of American values, American prestige at home and abroad, and an American sense of self and place.[11]

On Wednesday, August 19, 2009, a balding and slightly rotund William Calley spoke to the Kiwanis Club of Greater Columbus, Georgia, publically apologizing for the first time for his part in the My Lai Massacre. "There is not a day that goes by that I do not feel remorse for what happened that day in My Lai," he said, adding, "I feel remorse for the Vietnamese who were killed, for their families, for the American soldiers and their families. I am very sorry." He maintained, however, that he had simply followed orders.[12]

ACKNOWLEDGMENTS

SCHOLARS, JOURNALISTS, AND MANY OTHERS have written about My Lai. Early on-the-spot work of journalists such as Seymour Hersh, Richard Hammer, and others, who covered the story as it broke in 1969 as well as the subsequent investigations and trials, paved the way for later journalists and historians, among them Michael Bilton and Kevin Sim, Randy Roberts and James Olson, Michal Belknap, David Anderson, Edwin Moïse, and Kendrick Oliver, to explore either the totality or specific aspects of My Lai. Their work testifies to the importance of this tragedy to understanding the Vietnam War and its relevance to contemporary human values. I am sure I speak for all who study My Lai in giving these writers and scholars substantial thanks for their groundbreaking work.

I am also indebted to many wonderful people who helped bring this book to print. I am extremely grateful to Robert Brugger, a senior acquisitions editor at the Johns Hopkins University Press, and to Peter Charles Hoffer and Williamjames Hoffer, the editors for the Witness to History series, for inviting me to write this volume and for their constructive guidance throughout the entire process. Director Kathleen Keane and the fine folks at the Press, especially Julie McCarthy, Kara Reiter, Courtney Bond, and Josh Tong, are among the best in the business. A special thanks to copy editor Michael Baker, whose attention to detail, suggestions for clarity, and overall good writing sense made this a better book and me a better writer. He is a master of his craft.

Archivists and librarians at the Vietnam Center at Texas Tech University, the Army Center of Military History at Fort McNair, the National Archives at College Park, Maryland, the Muir Fairchild Library at Air University, the Zach S. Henderson Library at Georgia Southern University, and the Library of Congress, among others, as always offered more help than they realize. Colleagues at Georgia Southern University provided a steady stream of advice and feedback, especially on how they would use such a book in the classroom. The faculty at the US Air Force School of Advanced Air and Space Studies gave me an amazing year during my time as their Visiting Professor of Military History in 2010–11, during which, among other things, I worked on this book. Many friends and colleagues at these and other institutions were particularly helpful in their help and support. I especially want to thank and recognize Richard Boylan, Tim Nenninger, William Eckhardt, Raymond Ruhlmann, Tom Hughes, Hal Winton, Susan Matt, and Jennifer Whitton.

A special thanks to my dad, who served both as a Marine Corps lawyer and combat infantry officer in Vietnam during 1968–69, for, among many things, helping me get a sense both of combat operations and military justice issues from his perspective. Finally, to my partner in life, Jennifer, thank you for helping me work through the frustrations and celebrate the joys common to any project of this sort. I can never thank you enough for your help, support, and encouragement.

With full recognition of the assistance and support of those mentioned above, any omissions or errors are, of course, mine alone.

CHRONOLOGY

1946	French Indochina War begins
1954	France defeated by Ho Chi Minh's forces; Geneva Accords divide Vietnam at 17th parallel
1960	North Vietnam establishes National Liberation Front (NLF) in South Vietnam; the NLF becomes known as the Viet Cong, or Vietnamese communists
1962	Kennedy administration forms Military Assistance Command, Vietnam (MACV) to coordinate American advisory efforts to support South Vietnamese government and build South Vietnamese military
1964	Congress passes Tonkin Gulf Resolution, giving President Lyndon Johnson broad power to protect American citizens and interests in Southeast Asia
1965	Johnson administration "Americanizes" the war in Vietnam, taking over major combat operations from the South Vietnamese
1966	Captain Ernest Medina takes command of Charlie Company, 1st Battalion, 20th Infantry
1967	William Calley commissioned 2nd Lieutenant in US Army through OCS at Fort Benning; Charlie Company deployed to South Vietnam
January 26, 1968	Charlie Company assigned to Task Force Barker
January 30–31, 1968	Tet Offensive begins
February 25, 1968	Charlie Company enters minefield, losing three killed and twelve wounded
March 15, 1968	Task Force Barker issues orders for Son My operation
March 16, 1968	Members of Charlie Company and units of Task Force Barker murder hundreds of Vietnamese civilians in the village complex of Son My, notably My Lai (4)

March 16–18, 1968	Reports of killing of noncombatants reach various levels of Task Force Barker, 11th Infantry Brigade, and Americal Division command
March 28, 1968	Lieutenant Colonel Frank Barker submits after-action report for Son My operations; no mention of killing of noncombatants
April 24, 1968	Colonel Oran K. Henderson reports findings of informal investigation of alleged killing of noncombatants during Son My operation; he reports that twenty noncombatants were inadvertently killed by artillery and cross fire
March 29, 1969	Ronald Ridenhour, formerly of the 11th Infantry Brigade, sends letter to several members of congress and other officials in the US government detailing what he had heard about "My Lai"
April 23, 1969	Led by Colonel William Wilson, investigation of Army Inspector General into Ridenhour allegations begins
June 5, 1969	Lieutenant William Calley is reassigned to Fort Benning
June 9, 1969	Inspector General investigators question Calley in Washington
July 16, 1969	Paul Meadlo reveals to investigators that he and Calley murdered noncombatants on March 16, 1968
July 17, 1969	Colonel Wilson submits his report to the Inspector General, substantiating allegations of the killing of large numbers of noncombatants
August 4, 1969	Army CID takes over investigation
August 6, 1969	White House informed that reports indicate American soldiers may have killed large numbers of noncombatants on March 16, 1968, in Vietnam
September 5, 1969	Charges preferred against Lieutenant William Calley for murder of noncombatants the day before he is due to rotate out of the Army
October 22, 1969	Journalist Seymour Hersh begins investigating story that massacre may have occurred in Vietnam in March 1968
October 28, 1969	Charges preferred against Sergeant David Mitchell for assault to commit murder against thirty noncombatants on March 16, 1968

November 13, 1969	Seymour Hersh's story on My Lai appears in newspapers across the United States
November 20, 1969	Photographs of My Lai taken by Ronald Haeberle appear in the *Cleveland Plain Dealer*
November 24, 1969	Army appoints Lieutenant General William Peers to make initial investigations of My Lai incident; charges against Calley, including the murder of 109 noncombatants, referred to general court-martial at Fort Benning
December 5, 1969	*Life* magazine publishes photographic essay of Haeberle's pictures of My Lai
December 8, 1969	President Richard Nixon publically addresses My Lai for the first time, calling it an isolated incident
March 17, 1970	Results of Peers Inquiry announced at Pentagon press conference; includes allegations of dereliction against fourteen officers involved in covering up the My Lai incident, including Major General Samuel Koster
October 19, 1970	Mitchell court-martial begins
November 17, 1970	Calley court-martial begins
November 20, 1970	Mitchell acquitted of all charges
January 5, 1971	Court-martial of Sergeant Charles Hutto begins
January 14, 1971	Hutto acquitted of all charges
March 29, 1971	Calley found guilty of premeditated murder of no fewer than twenty-two Vietnamese civilians and of assault to commit murder of Vietnamese child
March 31, 1971	Calley sentenced to life imprisonment
April 26, 1971	Court-martial of Captain Eugene Kotouc begins
April 29, 1971	Kotouc acquitted of all charges
May 19, 1971	Secretary of the Army gives Major General Koster letter of censure, withdraws his Distinguished Service Medal, and reduces his rank to brigadier general
August 16, 1971	Court-martial of Captain Ernest Medina begins
August 18, 1971	Convening authority in Calley court-martial reduces confinement to twenty years
August 23, 1971	Court-martial of Colonel Oran K. Henderson begins
September 22, 1971	Medina acquitted of all charges
December 17, 1971	Henderson acquitted of all charges

January 27, 1973	United States and North Vietnam sign peace agreement, ending the American War in Vietnam
May 14, 1973	Calley denied clemency by the secretary of the Army
February 27, 1974	US District Court for the Middle District of Georgia orders Calley released on $1,000 personal bond
April 15, 1974	Secretary of the Army reduces Calley's confinement to ten years, making Calley eligible for parole in November 1974
May 3, 1974	President Nixon announces he will not intervene in the Calley case
June 13, 1974	US Court of Appeals for Fifth Circuit orders Calley returned to custody
August 8, 1974	Watergate scandal forces President Nixon to resign from office
September 25, 1974	District Court again orders Calley released from confinement pursuant to issuance of writ of habeas corpus
November 8, 1974	Court of Appeals orders Calley released on bail; secretary of the Army announces Calley's parole effective November 19, 1974
April 30, 1975	North Vietnamese forces take Saigon; Vietnam war ends
September 10, 1975	Court of Appeals reverses District Court decision to release Calley
September 11, 1975	Army announces it will not seek to return Calley to custody
1981	Army board rejects clemency for Calley
August 19, 2009	Calley speaks to Columbus, Georgia, Kiwanis Club, publically stating for the first time his "remorse" at what happened at My Lai, though he maintained he "was following orders"

NOTES

ABBREVIATIONS

1Lt.	first lieutenant
ARVN	Army of the Republic of Vietnam (South Vietnam)
CG	commanding general
CID	Criminal Investigation Division
CM	court-martial
CMA	Court of Military Appeals
CMR	Court of Military Review
Col. or COL	colonel
CWO	chief warrant officer
DFC	Distinguished Flying Cross
HQ	headquarters
IG	Inspector General
MACV	Military Assistance Command, Vietnam
NARA	National Archives and Records Administration, College Park, MD
PFC	private 1st class, enlisted rank
RG	record group
SP4, SP5	specialist 4th or 5th class, enlisted rank
SVN	South Vietnam
TF	task force
UCMJ	Uniform Code of Military Justice
USARV	United States Army, Vietnam
VATT	The Vietnam Archive, Texas Tech University

CHAPTER ONE: Charlie Company and Vietnam

1. Unless otherwise cited, material in this chapter is from testimony and reports included in *Report of the Department of the Army Review of the Preliminary Investigations into the My Lai Incident* (Washington, DC: Department of the Army, 1970), commonly referred to as the Peers Inquiry.

2. "Excerpts from Talk by Westmoreland," *New York Times* (November 22, 1967): 2.

3. The following discussion on the war in Vietnam is taken from Christian G.

Appy, *Working-Class War: American Combat Soldiers and Vietnam* (Chapel Hill: University of North Carolina Press, 1993); Guenter Lewy, *America in Vietnam* (Oxford: Oxford University Press, 1978); Andrew F. Krepinevich, *The Army and Vietnam* (Baltimore: Johns Hopkins University Press, 1986); James R. Ebert, *A Life in a Year: The American Infantryman in Vietnam, 1965–1972* (Novato, CA: Presidio Press, 1993); Ronald H. Spector, *After Tet: The Bloodiest Year in Vietnam* (New York: Vintage, 1993); James E. Westheider, *The Vietnam War* (Westport, CT: Greenwood Press, 2007); and Lewis Sorley, *Westmoreland: The General Who Lost Vietnam* (Boston: Houghton Mifflin Harcourt, 2011).

4. Philip Caputo, *A Rumor of War* (New York: Ballantine, 1977), 6.

5. Michael Bilton and Kevin Sim, *Four Hours in My Lai* (New York: Penguin, 1992), 11.

6. Michal R. Belknap, *The Vietnam War on Trial: The My Lai Massacre and the Court-Martial of Lieutenant William Calley* (Lawrence: University Press of Kansas, 2002), 27.

7. D. Michael Shafer, *The Legacy: The Vietnam War in the American Imagination* (Boston: Beacon, 1990), 100.

8. Appy, *Working-Class War,* 201, 267; Nick Turse, "The Doctrine of Atrocity: Us against 'Them'—A Tradition of Institutionalized Brutality," *Village Voice* (May 4, 2004); John A. Parrish, *12, 20, & 5: A Doctor's Year in Vietnam* (New York: Dutton, 1972), 316.

9. US Army, Field Manual 27–10: *The Law of Land Warfare* (Washington, DC: Government Printing Office, 1956), esp. 505(d) and 507(b); UCMJ, Title 10, US Code, esp. Articles 18 and 21; William G. Eckhardt, "My Lai, an American Tragedy," *UMKC Law Review* 68 (Summer 2000): 677–78.

10. UCMJ, Articles 90 and 92.

11. US Department of Defense, *Manual for Courts-Martial, United States* (Washington, DC: Government Printing Office, 1969).

12. *The Law of Land Warfare,* 509(a).

13. Exhibit D-17, USARV Regulation 350-1, "Education and Training," November 10, 1967, Peers Inquiry, Vol. 3, Bk. 1; Exhibit D-18, USARV Regulation 612-1, "Personnel Processing: Issue and Possession of Information Cards," January 8, 1968, Peers Inquiry, Vol. 3, Bk. 1.

14. Exhibit M-94, "Code of Conduct for Members of the Armed Forces of the United States," Peers Inquiry, Vol. 3, Bk. 1.

15. Exhibit M-94, "The Enemy in Your Hands," Peers Inquiry, Vol. 3, Bk. 1.

16. Exhibit M-94, "Nine Rules for Personnel of the U.S. Military Assistance Command, Vietnam," Peers Inquiry, Vol. 3, Bk. 1.

17. Exhibit D-45, "Guidance for Commanders in Vietnam," Peers Inquiry, Vol. 3, Bk. 1.

18. Exhibit D-6, MACV Directive 525-3, "Combat Operations: Minimizing Noncombatant Battle Casualties," October 14, 1966, Peers Inquiry, Vol. 3, Bk. 1.

19. Exhibit D-40, MACV Directive 525-9, "Combat Operations: Control, Disposition, and Safeguarding of Vietnamese Property, Captured Material, and Food Supplies," April 10, 1967, Peers Inquiry, Vol. 3, Bk. 1.

20. Exhibit D-39, MACV Directive 381-46, "Military Intelligence: Combined Screening of Detainees," December 27, 1967, Peers Inquiry, Vol. 3, Bk. 1; Exhibit D-43, MACV Directive 190-3, "Military Police: Enemy Prisoners of War," February 15, 1968, Peers Inquiry, Vol. 3, Bk. 1.

21. Exhibit D-1, MACV Directive 20-4, "Inspections and Investigations: War Crimes," April 27, 1967, Peers Inquiry, Vol. 3, Bk. 1; Exhibit D-38, MACV Directive 27-5, "Legal Services, War Crimes, and Other Prohibited Acts," November 2, 1967, Peers Inquiry, Vol. 3, Bk. 1.

22. Exhibit D-10, USARV Regulation 335-6, "Serious Incident Reports," June 24, 1967, Peers Inquiry, Vol. 3, Bk. 1; Exhibit D-8, MACV Directive 335-1, "Reports: Reports of Serious Crimes or Incidents," November 22, 1967, Peers Inquiry, Vol. 3, Bk. 1.

23. Exhibit D-2, Army Regulation 15-6, "Procedures for Investigating Officers and Boards of Officers Conducting Investigations," August 12, 1966, Peers Inquiry, Vol. 3, Bk. 1.

24. George S. Prugh, *Law at War: Vietnam, 1964–1973* (Washington, DC: Department of the Army, 1975), 72–78.

25. John Miller, Jr., *The United States Army in World War II: The Army in the Pacific–Guadalcanal: The First Offensive* (Washington, DC: US Army Center of Military History, 1995), 213–16.

26. John B. Wilson, *Maneuver and Firepower: The Evolution of Divisions and Separate Brigades* (Washington, DC: US Army Center of Military History, 1998), 325–34.

27. "Americal Combat Center Lesson Plan, Geneva Convention," DF, AVDF-JA, 18 December 1967: Instruction on Hague and Geneva Conventions, RG 472, Records of US Forces in Southeast Asia, 23rd Infantry Division, Box 4, Folder 23, NARA; Exhibit D-14, Investigation of Artillery Incidents, January 15, 1968, Peers Inquiry, Vol. 3, Bk. 2.

28. Bilton and Sim, *Four Hours in My Lai*, 54.

29. Ibid., 87.

30. Initiated under Secretary of Defense Robert McNamara, Project 100,000 intended to enlist 100,000 men from inner city and poorer neighborhoods with aptitude scores below the norm, with the intent to provide vocational training to improve their job prospects upon rotating out of service. Far from being a jobs training program, however, Project 100,000 sent many enlistees to Vietnam, without giving them the requisite vocational training. See Lewy, *America in Vietnam*, 331, and Janice H. Laurence and Peter F. Ramsberger, *Low-Aptitude Men in the Military: Who Profits? Who Pays?* (New York: Praeger, 1991).

31. Fact Sheet, Company C, 1st Battalion, 20th Infantry, January 12, 1970, RG 319, Records of the Army Staff, Records Pertaining to My Lai, Box 1, My Lai Staff Summaries, January 1970, NARA.

32. Belknap, *The Vietnam War on Trial,* 37–38; Fact Sheet, Company C, 1st Battalion, 20th Infantry, December 21, 1969, RG 319, Records Pertaining to My Lai, Box 1, My Lai Staff Summaries, January 1970, NARA.

33. Belknap, *The Vietnam War on Trial,* 27–36; Richard Hammer, *One Morning in the War: The Tragedy at Son My* (New York: Coward-McCann, 1970), 74–77.

34. John Sack, *Lieutenant Calley: His Own Story* (New York: Grosset & Dunlap, 1970), 29.

35. Hammer, *One Morning in the War,* 87–89.

36. Ibid., 96–97.

37. Bernd Greiner, *War without Fronts: The USA in Vietnam,* translated from the German by Anne Wyburd with Victoria Fern (New Haven: Yale University Press, 2009), 201–2.

38. Sack, *Lieutenant Calley,* 52–56; Belknap, *The Vietnam War on Trial,* 54–55.

39. Richard Hammer, *The Court-Martial of Lieutenant Calley* (New York: Coward, McCann, & Geoghegan, 1971), 304–5; Sack, *Lieutenant Calley,* 71–73.

40. Sack, *Lieutenant Calley,* 73.

CHAPTER TWO: March 16, 1968

1. United States v. Calley, 46 CMR 1131 (ACMR 1973), in Joseph Goldstein, Burke Marshall, and Jack Schwartz, eds., *The My Lai Massacre and Its Cover-Up: Beyond the Reach of the Law?* (New York: Free Press, 1976), 494. Unless otherwise cited, material in this chapter is from testimony and reports included in *Report of the Department of the Army Review of the Preliminary Investigations into the My Lai Incident* (Washington, DC: Department of the Army, 1970), commonly referred to as the Peers Inquiry.

2. Combat After Action Report (RCS AVDF-GC1), Task Force Barker, 11th Infantry Brigade, Americal Division, 28 March 1968, RG 472, Records of US Forces in Southeast Asia, 23rd Infantry Division, Inspector General, Command Reports, My Lai (4) Investigation, Box 1, Folder 1, NARA.

3. Richard Hammer, *The Court-Martial of Lt. Calley* (New York: Coward, McCann & Geoghegan, 1971), 245–46.

4. John Sack, *Lieutenant Calley: His Own Story* (New York: Viking, 1971), 98.

5. Ibid., 98–99.

6. Michael Bilton and Kevin Sim, *Four Hours in My Lai* (New York: Penguin, 1992), 104–5; CID Investigation Report—My Lai, 25 September 1970, RG 319, Records of the Army Staff, Records Pertaining to My Lai (4), Box 6, Case Folder: 1Lt. William L. Calley, Jr., [Part 4 of 4], NARA.

7. Task Force Barker Log, 16 March 1968; Peers Inquiry, Vol. 3, Bk. 3.

8. CID Investigation Report—My Lai, 25 September 1970, RG 319, Records Pertaining to My Lai (4), Box 6, Case Folder: 1Lt. William L. Calley, Jr., [Part 4 of 4], NARA.

9. Ibid.

10. CID Statements Reference Hutto and (or) Schiel, No Date, Folder 28, Box

02, My Lai Collection, VATT; CID Report of Investigation, 4 September 1970, Folder 14, Box 02, My Lai Collection, VATT.

11. CID Report of Investigation, 26 June 1970, Folder 14, Box 02, My Lai Collection, VATT.

12. CID Report of Investigation, 20 January 1970, Folder 14, Box 02, My Lai Collection, VATT.

13. CID Report of Investigation, 26 June 1970, Folder 14, Box 02, My Lai Collection, VATT.

14. Statement by accused or suspected person (Harry Stanley), 14 October 1969, Folder 47, Box 01, My Lai Collection, VATT; CID Investigation Report—My Lai, 25 September 1970, RG 319, Records Pertaining to My Lai (4), Box 6, Case Folder: 1Lt. William L. Calley, Jr., [Part 4 of 4], NARA.

15. Witness Statement (Robert Maples), 18 September 1969, Folder 47, Box 01, My Lai Collection, VATT; Bilton and Sim, *Four Hours in My Lai,* 111.

16. Sack, *Lieutenant Calley,* 107–9; Michal R. Belknap, *The Vietnam War on Trial: The My Lai Massacre and the Court-Martial of Lieutenant William Calley* (Lawrence: University Press of Kansas, 2002), 70.

17. Testimony of Mr. Paul D. Meadlo taken by Colonel William V. Wilson, IG, 16 July 1969, Folder 21, Box 01, My Lai Collection, VATT; CID Investigation Report—My Lai, 25 September 1970, RG 319, Records Pertaining to My Lai (4), Box 6, Case Folder: 1Lt. William L. Calley, Jr., [Part 4 of 4], NARA.

18. CID Investigation Report—My Lai, 25 September 1970, RG 319, Records Pertaining to My Lai (4), Box 6, Case Folder: 1Lt. William L. Calley, Jr., [Part 4 of 4], NARA; Belknap, *The Vietnam War on Trial,* 72–73.

19. Bilton and Sim, *Four Hours in My Lai,* 123.

20. Statement by accused or suspected person (Harry Stanley), 14 October 1969, Folder 47, Box 01, My Lai Collection, VATT.

21. 11th Infantry Brigade Journal, 14–18 March 1968, Peers Inquiry, Vol. 3, Bk. 3.

22. Trent Angers, *The Forgotten Hero of My Lai: The Hugh Thompson Story* (Lafayette, LA: Acadian House, 1999), 114.

23. Ibid., 118–21.

24. Aviator's (CWO Thompson) statement, RG 319, Records Pertaining to My Lai (4), Box 1, Personnel Involved in My Lai Incident, NARA; Angers, *Forgotten Hero,* 128–31; Testimony of PFC Lawrence M. Colburn taken by Colonel William V. Wilson, IG, 19 June 1969, Folder 17, Box 01, My Lai Collection, VATT.

25. Aviator's (CWO Thompson) statement, RG 319, Records Pertaining to My Lai (4), Box 1, Personnel Involved in My Lai Incident, NARA; Angers, *Forgotten Hero,* 128–31; Testimony of PFC Lawrence M. Colburn taken by Colonel William V. Wilson, IG, 19 June 1969, Folder 17, Box 01, My Lai Collection, VATT.

26. Testimony of Frederick J. Widmer taken by William V. Wilson, 15 July 1969, Folder 20, Box 01, My Lai Collection, VATT; Bilton and Sim, *Four Hours in My Lai,* 128–29.

27. Exhibit M-109, HQ 11th Inf. Bde. Letter, Subject: PFC Carter, with Casualty Report, 6 April 1968, Peers Inquiry, Vol. 3, Bk. 4.

28. CID Statements Reference Hutto and (or) Schiel, No Date, Folder 28, Box 02, My Lai Collection, VATT.

29. Witness Statement (Dennis Bunning), 7 December 1969, Folder 49, Box 01, My Lai Collection, VATT; Bilton and Sim, *Four Hours in My Lai,* 128–31.

30. CID Investigation Report—My Lai, 25 September 1970, RG 319, Records Pertaining to My Lai (4), Box 6, Case Folder: 1Lt. William L. Calley, Jr. [Part 4 of 4], 21–22, NARA.

31. Testimony of Mr. John H. Paul, 16 June 1969, Folder 15, Box 01, My Lai Collection, VATT.

32. Exhibit M-85, Diary Extracts of Thomas Partsch, 15–18 March 1968, Peers Inquiry, Vol. 3, Bk. 4.

33. Exhibit M-21, Captain Livingston's Letter to His Wife, 16 March 1968, Peers Inquiry, Vol. 3, Bk. 4.

CHAPTER THREE: Aftermath

1. Task Force Barker Log, 14–18 March 1968, Peers Inquiry, Vol. 3, Bk. 3. Unless otherwise cited, material and quotes in this chapter are from testimony and reports included in *Report of the Department of the Army Review of the Preliminary Investigations into the My Lai Incident* (Washington, DC: Department of the Army, 1970), commonly referred to as the Peers Inquiry.

2. CID Investigation Report—My Lai, 25 September 1970, RG 319, Records of the Army Staff, Records Pertaining to My Lai (4), Box 6, Case Folder: 1Lt. William L. Calley, Jr., [Part 4 of 4], NARA.

3. Witness statement of Pham Thi Don, 29 December 1969, Folder 52, Box 01, My Lai Collection, VATT.

4. CID Investigation Report—My Lai, 25 September 1970, RG 319, Records Pertaining to My Lai (4), Box 6, Case Folder: 1Lt. William L. Calley, Jr., [Part 4 of 4], NARA.

5. Witness Statement, 18 September 1969, Folder 47, Box 01, My Lai Collection, VATT.

6. Richard Hammer, *One Morning in the War: The Tragedy of Son My* (New York: Coward-McCann, 1970), 160–61; Seymour Hersh, *Cover-Up: The Army's Secret Investigation of the Massacre at My Lai 4* (New York: Random House, 1972), 141–44.

7. Hammer, *One Morning in the War,* 160–61; Hersh, *Cover-Up,* 142.

8. Exhibit D-34, Fragmented Order 24-68, Disbanding TF Barker, April 1968, Peers Inquiry, Vol. 3, Bk. 2.

9. The following material on the initial reports and subsequent cover-up is from Peers Inquiry, Vol. 1, Hersh, *Cover-Up,* and Michael Bilton and Kevin Sim, *Four Hours in My Lai* (New York: Penguin, 1992).

10. Hersh, *Cover-Up,* 138.

11. Ibid., 135–36.

12. Bilton and Sim, *Four Hours in My Lai,* 178–80.

13. TF Barker After-Action Report, 28 March 1968, Box 1, Folder 1, 23rd Infantry Division, Inspector General, Command Reports, My Lai (4) Investigation, RG 472, Records of US Forces in Southeast Asia, NARA.

14. Exhibit M-58, Release No. 113-68-75, Info Office, 11th Infantry Bde., by SP5 Jay A. Roberts, Peers Inquiry, Vol. 3, Bk. 4.

15. Exhibit M-60, *Americal News Sheet,* 18 March 1968, Peers Inquiry, Vol. 3, Bk. 4, Exhibit M-88, *Stars and Stripes,* 18 March 1968 (Extract, page 6), Peers Inquiry, Vol. 3, Bk. 4; William C. Westmoreland, *A Soldier Reports* (New York: Da Capo, 1989), 375–76.

16. "G.I.'s, in Pincer Move, Kill 128 in Day Long Battle," *New York Times* (March 17, 1968): 1.

17. Exhibit M-131, Census Grievance Committee Report, 18 March 1968, Peers Inquiry, Vol. 3, Bk. 4.

18. Exhibit M-49, Mr. Do Dinh's Letter to District Chief, Son Tinh District, 22 March 1968, Subj.: Report of the Allied Operation, 16 March 1968, Peers Inquiry, Vol. 3, Bk. 4.

19. Exhibit M-28, Lieutenant Tan's letter to Colonel Khien, Quang Ngai Province Chief, 28 March 1968, Peers Inquiry, Vol. 3, Bk. 4.

20. Exhibit M-29, Lieutenant Tan's Letter to Province Chief, 11 April 1968, Peers Inquiry, Vol. 3, Bk. 4.

21. Exhibit M-35, VC Propaganda Leaflet, Dated 28 March 1968, Peers Inquiry, Vol. 3, Bk. 4.

22. Exhibit M-33, VC Propaganda Broadcast, an Inclosure [*sic*] to Memo to CG, 2nd ARVN Div., Peers Inquiry, Vol. 3, Bk. 4.

23. Exhibit M-36, Memo for COL, CG, 2nd ARVN Div., 12 April 1968, Peers Inquiry, Vol. 3, Bk. 4.

24. Exhibit M-30, Signed Statement by Angel M. Rodriguez, 14 April 1968, Peers Inquiry, Vol. 3, Bk. 4.

25. Exhibit R-1, Col. Henderson's "Report of Investigation," 24 April 1968, Peers Inquiry, Vol. 3, Bk. 3.

26. General Orders Number 3601, Award of the Distinguished Flying Cross, 1 July 1968, DFC for Hugh Thompson, 1 July 1968, RG 472, 23rd Infantry Division, Box 2, Folder 7, NARA.

27. Bronze Star citation for SP4 Lawrence Colburn, Aero-Scout Company, 123rd Aviation Battalion, 4 August 1968, RG 472, 23rd Infantry Division, Box 3, Folder 13, NARA; Bronze Star citation for E3 Glenn Andreotta, 123rd Aviation Battalion, 24 August 1968, RG 472, 23rd Infantry Division, Box 5, Folder 26, NARA. Andreotta was killed on April 8, 1968, when the helicopter in which he was a crewmember was hit by enemy fire.

28. Trent Angers, *The Forgotten Hero of My Lai: The Hugh Thompson Story* (Lafayette, LA: Acadian House, 1999), 18–19. On March 6, 1998, the Army awarded Thompson, Colburn, and Andreotta (posthumously) the Soldier's Medal, the highest award for bravery not involving conflict with enemy forces, in a ceremony at the

Vietnam Veterans Memorial in Washington, DC. See "3 Honored for Saving Lives at My Lai," *New York Times* (March 7, 1998): A9.

CHAPTER FOUR: Discovery

1. Unless otherwise cited, material in this chapter is from testimony and reports included in *Report of the Department of the Army Review of the Preliminary Investigations into the My Lai Incident* (Washington, DC: Department of the Army, 1970), commonly referred to as the Peers Inquiry.
2. Exhibit M-83, Letter from Mr. Ronald Ridenhour, 29 March 1969, Peers Inquiry, Vol. 3, Bk. 4; Michael Bilton and Kevin Sim, *Four Hours in My Lai* (New York: Viking, 1992), 218–20.
3. Testimony of William C. Westmoreland, June 10, 1970, *Investigation of the My Lai Incident, Hearings of the Armed Services Investigating Subcommittee of the Committee on Armed Services, House of Representatives, 91st Congress, 2nd Session* (Washington, DC: Government Printing Office, 1976), 832; William C. Westmoreland, *A Soldier Reports* (New York: Doubleday, 1976), 456.
4. Exhibit M-98, HQ-USARV, Memo for Record, Subj: Inquiry Concerning Alleged Massacre, My Lai, 17 April 1969, Peers Inquiry, Vol. 3, Bk. 4.
5. William V. Wilson, "I Had Prayed to God that This Thing Was Fiction," *American Heritage* (February 1990): 46.
6. Ibid., 49–52; Testimony of SGT E-5 Michael A. Bernhardt, 8 May 1969, Folder 04, Box 01, My Lai Collection, VATT.
7. Testimony of PFC Lawrence Colburn, 19 June 1969, Folder 17, Box 01, My Lai Collection, VATT; Wilson, "I Had Prayed to God that This Thing Was Fiction," 49–52; Trent Angers, *The Forgotten Hero of My Lai: The Hugh Thompson Story* (Lafayette, LA: Acadian House, 1999), 155–57.
8. Testimony of 1Lt. William Calley, Jr., 9 June 1969, Folder 13, Box 01, My Lai Collection, VATT.
9. Aviator's (CWO Thompson) Report, RG 319, Records of the Army Staff, Records Pertaining to My Lai (4), Box 1, Personnel Involved in My Lai Incident, NARA.
10. Testimony of Mr. Paul D. Meadlo, 16 July 1969, Folder 21, Box 01, My Lai Collection, VATT.
11. Wilson, "I Had Prayed to God that This Thing Was Fiction," 53.
12. Bilton and Sim, *Four Hours in My Lai*, 240–42.
13. Witness Statement, 24 November 1969, Folder 62, Box 04, My Lai Collection, VATT; Bilton and Sim, *Four Hours in My Lai*, 273–75.
14. Directive for Investigation, 26 November 1969, Peers Inquiry, Vol. 1, 1–6.
15. William C. Westmoreland, *A Soldier Reports* (New York: Doubleday, 1976), 376; Lewis Sorley, *Westmoreland: The General Who Lost Vietnam* (Boston: Houghton Mifflin Harcourt, 2011), 214.
16. Seymour Hersh, *My Lai 4: A Report on the Massacre and Its Aftermath* (New York: Random House, 1970), 229–30; "Army's Investigator: William Ray Peers," *New*

York Times (March 18, 1970): 14; William R. Peers, *The My Lai Inquiry* (New York: Norton, 1979), 3–11, 49–51.

17. Peers, *My Lai Inquiry*, 7, 199; "Army Inquiry Charges 14 Officers in Suppression of Songmy Facts," *New York Times* (March 18, 1970): 1, 14.

18. Hersh, *My Lai 4*, 128; "Army Accuses Lieutenant in Vietnam Deaths in 1968," *New York Times* (September 7, 1969): 14.

19. Bilton and Sim, *Four Hours in My Lai*, 250; Hersh, *My Lai 4*, 132–33; Seymour Hersh, "How I Broke the My Lai 4 Story," *Saturday Review* (May 30, 1970): 23–25.

20. Bilton and Sim, *Four Hours in My Lai*, 251; Hersh, *My Lai 4*, 133–35; Hersh, "How I Broke the My Lai 4 Story," 23–25; "Miscue on the Massacre," *Time* (December 5, 1969): 75.

21. Bilton and Sim, *Four Hours in My Lai*, 261–64; Hersh, *My Lai 4*, 138–41; Hersh, "How I Broke the My Lai 4 Story," 23–25; Ronald Haeberle and Joseph Eszterhas, "The Massacre at My Lai," *Life* (December 5, 1969): 36–45; "Resor Called to Testify about Alleged Massacre," *New York Times* (November 26, 1969): 1, 10.

22. "G.I.'s Near Songmy Doubt Any Massacre," *New York Times* (December 1, 1969): 12.

23. "Talk of the Town: Notes and Comment," *New Yorker* (December 20, 1969): 27–29.

24. "The Lesson of Pinkville," *Christianity Today* (December 19, 1969): 23.

25. "Self-Respect after My Lai," *Christian Century* (December 10, 1969): 1569.

26. John Osborne, "Death to Gooks," *New Republic* (December 13, 1969): 17–18. Emphasis in the original.

27. "On Evil: The Inescapable Fact," *Time* (December 5, 1969): 26–27.

28. "The American Conscience," *Nation* (December 8, 1969): 619–20.

29. "The Great Atrocity Hunt," *National Review* (December 16, 1969): 1252.

30. "Nixon's Own Words," *U.S. News & World Report* (December 22, 1969): 48–49; "President's News Conference of December 8, 1969," *Department of State Bulletin*, (December 29, 1969): 617–18.

31. Rick Perlstein, *Nixonland: The Rise of a President and the Fracturing of America* (New York: Scribner, 2008), 441–44; "A Time–Louis Harris Poll: The War: New Support for Nixon," *Time* (January 12, 1970): 16.

32. "Resor Called to Testify about Alleged Massacre," *New York Times* (November 26, 1969): 1, 10.

33. Quoted in Hersh, *My Lai 4*, 157–58.

34. "White House Says U.S. Policy Bars Any Mass Slaying," *New York Times* (November 27, 1969): 1, 18.

35. Hersh, *My Lai 4*, 167–69; various, *New York Times* (December 9–13, 1969).

36. See *Investigation of the My Lai Incident*, and *Report of the Armed Services Investigating Subcommittee of the Committee on Armed Services, 91st Congress, House of Representatives, 2nd Session, July 15, 1970* (Washington, DC: Government Printing Office, 1970); Angers, *Forgotten Hero*, 155–70.

37. Stanley R. Resor to F. Edward Hébert, January 6, 1970, Resor-Hébert Cor-

respondence, RG 319, Records Pertaining to the My Lai (4) Investigation, Box 1, My Lai Army Staff Summaries, January 1970, NARA. For the Jencks Act, see 18 U.S.C. §3500. Congress passed the Jencks Act in 1957 in response to the conviction of Clinton Jencks, a labor organizer, of being a member of the Communist Party despite the government's failure to produce documents that prosecution witnesses cited as evidence. The Supreme Court overturned Jencks's conviction because the government failed to produce documents in support of prosecution witness testimony. See Jencks v. United States 353 U.S. 657 (1957).

38. Mark D. Carson, "F. Edward Hébert and the Congressional Investigation of the My Lai Massacre," *Louisiana History* 37, no. 1 (Winter 1996): 61–79; Michal R. Belknap, *The Vietnam War on Trial: The My Lai Massacre and the Court-Martial of Lieutenant Calley* (Lawrence: University Press of Kansas, 2002), 141–43, 222–24; William G. Eckhardt, "My Lai: An American Tragedy," *UMKC Law Review* 68 (Summer 2000): 684–86.

39. Report of Colonel Tan That Khien, Commander, Quang Ngai Province, 20 November 1969, RG 472, Records of US Forces in Southeast Asia, Americal Division, IG Investigation My Lai (4), Box 13, NARA.

40. SVN Investigation, My Lai (1969), RG 472, Americal Division, Box 10, Folder 53, NARA.

41. Belknap, *The Vietnam War on Trial*, 130–32.

42. Fact Sheet, Court-Martial of First Lieutenant William Calley, RG 319, Records Pertaining to Calley Court-Martial, Box 6, My Lai Lessons Learned Folder, NARA.

43. "Army Consolidating Songmy Inquiry at Georgia Base," *New York Times* (January 14, 1970): 5.

44. "Sonmy Trial Is Snarled by House Panel's Refusal to Divulge 4 Men's Testimony," *New York Times* (October 16, 1970): 12; "G.I. in My Lai Case Cleared by Army," *New York Times* (November 21, 1970): 1, 13; Belknap, *The Vietnam War on Trial*, 223–25.

45. Statement by Accused or Suspect Person, 17 November 1969, Folder 48, Box 01, My Lai Collection, VATT.

46. "Army Clears Hutto in Deaths at My Lai," *New York Times* (January 15, 1971): 1, 7; Belknap, *The Vietnam War on Trial*, 225–26; Bilton and Sim, *Four Hours in My Lai*, 329–30.

47. Fact Sheet, Court-Martial of First Lieutenant William Calley, RG 319, Records Pertaining to Calley Court-Martial, Box 6, My Lai Lessons Learned Folder, NARA; "Army Clears G.I.'s in My Lai Killing," *New York Times* (January 23, 1971): 15; Belknap, *The Vietnam War on Trial*, 226–27.

CHAPTER FIVE: Trial

1. Arthur Everett, Kathryn Johnson, and Harry F. Rosenthal, *Calley* (New York: Dell, 1971), 120; Richard Hammer, *The Court-Martial of Lt. Calley* (New York: Coward, McCann, & Geoghegan, 1971), 39.

2. Michal R. Belknap, *The Vietnam War on Trial: The My Lai Massacre and the Court-Martial of Lieutenant Calley* (Lawrence: University Press of Kansas, 2002), 146–47; Hammer, *The Court-Martial of Lt. Calley*, 74.

3. Hammer, *The Court-Martial of Lt. Calley*, 66–68, 81–84.

4. "U.S. Details Case against Calley," *New York Times* (November 18, 1970): 1, 15; Hammer, *The Court-Martial of Lt. Calley*, 75–79, 80–81.

5. "Ex-G.I. Says He Witnessed Slaying of Unarmed Civilians but Did Not See Calley," *New York Times* (November 19, 1970): 13; "Mylai Panel told of Shots at Dead," *New York Times* (November 21, 1970): 13; "Two Mylai Witnesses Say Citations Were False," *New York Times* (November 24, 1970): 8.

6. "Trial of Calley Told of Strafing," *New York Times* (November 25, 1970): 21; Belknap, *The Vietnam War on Trial*, 157–59; Hammer, *The Court-Martial of Lt. Calley*, 85–108.

7. "Witness Says Calley Shot at Mylai Civilians," *New York Times* (December 2, 1970): 1, 14; Belknap, *The Vietnam War on Trial*, 160–61; Hammer, *The Court-Martial of Lt. Calley*, 110–15.

8. "A Calley Witness Refuses Answers," *New York Times* (December 3, 1970): 10; Belknap, *The Vietnam War on Trial*, 161–62; Hammer, *The Court-Martial of Lt. Calley*, 116–18.

9. "Ex-G.I. Taken into Custody after Refusing to Testify at Calley Trial," *New York Times* (December 4, 1970): 4; Hammer, *The Court-Martial of Lt. Calley*, 118–21.

10. "Ex-G.I. Says Calley Killed Non-Resistors," *New York Times* (December 5, 1970): 1, 13; "Witness Testifies Calley Shot Civilians at Mylai for an Hour," *New York Times* (December 8, 1970): 1, 12; "U.S. Rests Case against Calley," *New York Times* (December 9, 1970); 21; Belknap, *The Vietnam War on Trial*, 162–63; Hammer, *The Court-Martial of Lt. Calley*, 129–47.

11. "Defense Says Calley Acted under Orders," *New York Times* (December 10, 1970): 4; "Calley's Lawyer Explains Actions," *New York Times* (December 11, 1970): 9; Hammer, *The Court-Martial of Lt. Calley*, 177–79.

12. "Calley's Lawyer Explains Actions," *New York Times* (December 11, 1970): 9; Hammer, *The Court-Martial of Lt. Calley*, 177–80.

13. "5 Recall 'Impression' Medina Wanted Everyone at Mylai Killed," *New York Times* (December 15, 1970): 10; "Medina Accused at Calley Trial," *New York Times* (December 16, 1970): 1; Hammer, *The Court-Martial of Lt. Calley*, 184–93.

14. Hammer, *The Court-Martial of Lt. Calley*, 194–95.

15. "Ex-G.I. Says He and Calley Shot Civilians at Mylai under Orders," *New York Times* (January 12, 1971): 12; Hammer, *The Court-Martial of Lt. Calley*, 148–52.

16. "Ex-G.I. Says He and Calley Shot Civilians at Mylai under Orders," *New York Times* (January 12, 1971): 1, 12; "Mylai G.I. Feared Babies Held Grenades," *New York Times* (January 13, 1971): 4; Hammer, *The Court-Martial of Lt. Calley*, 152–63.

17. "Calley Trial Recessed for Psychiatric Test," *New York Times* (January 19, 1971): 4; Belknap, *The Vietnam War on Trial*, 172.

18. "Calley Trial Recessed for Psychiatric Test," *New York Times* (January 19,

1971): 4; Belknap, *The Vietnam War on Trial,* 172–73; Hammer, *The Court-Martial of Lt. Calley,* 215–21.

19. "Calley Calls Mental Tests an 'Unwarranted' Measure," *New York Times* (January 27, 1971): 4; "Sanity Unit Finds Calley 'Normal,'" *New York Times* (February 17, 1971): 8; Hammer, *The Court-Martial of Lt. Calley,* 222–26.

20. "Two Doctors Say Calley Lacked Ability to Premeditate Slayings," *New York Times* (February 19, 1971): 6; Belknap, *The Vietnam War on Trial,* 174; Hammer, *The Court-Martial of Lt. Calley,* 222–29.

21. "Two Doctors Say Calley Lacked Ability to Premeditate Slayings," *New York Times* (February 19, 1971): 6.

22. "Psychiatrist Ousted as Calley Witness and All of His Testimony Is Expunged," *New York Times* (February 20, 1971): 10; Hammer, *The Court-Martial of Lt. Calley,* 229–35.

23. "Calley on Stand, Tells of Hatred," *New York Times* (February 23, 1971): 1, 12; Hammer, *The Court-Martial of Lt. Calley,* 234–38; Belknap, *The Vietnam War on Trial,* 175–76.

24. "Doctor, Assume the Following to Be True," *New York Times* (February 21, 1971): E2; "Calley on Stand, Tells of Hatred," *New York Times* (February 23, 1971): 1, 12; Hammer, *The Court-Martial of Lt. Calley,* 238.

25. "Calley on Stand, Tells of Hatred," *New York Times* (February 23, 1971): 1, 12; Hammer, *The Court-Martial of Lt. Calley,* 239–44.

26. "Calley Concedes Killings: Says He Acted on Orders," *New York Times* (February 24, 1971): 1, 20; "Excerpts from Calley Testimony on Mylai Killings," *New York Times* (February 24, 1971): 20; Hammer, *The Court-Martial of Lt. Calley,* 245–46.

27. "Excerpts from Calley Testimony on Mylai Killings," *New York Times* (February 24, 1971): 20; Hammer, *The Court-Martial of Lt. Calley,* 249–54.

28. "Excerpts from Calley Testimony on Mylai Killings," *New York Times* (February 24, 1971): 20; Hammer, *The Court-Martial of Lt. Calley,* 255–59.

29. Hammer, *The Court-Martial of Lt. Calley,* 260.

30. "Calley Says He Never Questioned Mylai Orders," *New York Times* (February 25, 1971): 1, 24; "Calley Testimony Excerpts," *New York Times* (February 25, 1971): 24; Hammer, *The Court-Martial of Lt. Calley,* 260–73.

31. "Calley Says He Never Questioned Mylai Orders," *New York Times* (February 25, 1971): 1, 24; "Calley Testimony Excerpts," *New York Times* (February 25, 1971): 24; Hammer, *The Court-Martial of Lt. Calley,* 271–73.

32. "Calley Says He Never Questioned Mylai Orders," *New York Times* (February 25, 1971): 1, 24; Hammer, *The Court-Martial of Lt. Calley,* 279–81.

33. "Calley Says He Never Questioned Mylai Orders," *New York Times* (February 25, 1971): 1, 24; Hammer, *The Court-Martial of Lt. Calley,* 281–82.

34. "Slaying Order Denied," *New York Times* (March 6, 1971): 6; "Prompt Reports on Mylai Cited," *New York Times* (March 4, 1971): 6; "Mylai Inquiry Ban Is Laid to General," *New York Times* (March 5, 1971): 1, 13; "Calley Trial Told of Death in Well," *New York Times* (March 9, 1971): 7; Hammer, *The Court-Martial of Lt. Calley,* 288–92.

35. "Last Calley Witness Says Mylai Troops Went to Vietnam Unready for Combat," *New York Times* (March 12, 1971): 17; Hammer, *The Court-Martial of Lt. Calley,* 296–97, 324–27; Belknap, *The Vietnam War on Trial,* 180.

36. Hammer, *The Court-Martial of Lt. Calley,* 299–300.

37. "Excerpts from Testimony of Captain Medina at Court-Martial of Lieutenant Calley," *New York Times* (March 11, 1971): 24; "Medina Rejects Calley Account," *New York Times* (March 11, 1971): 1, 24; Hammer, *The Court-Martial of Lt. Calley,* 300–323; Belknap, *The Vietnam War on Trial,* 182–83.

38. "Calley Case Goes to Military Jury," *New York Times* (March 17, 1971): 1, 20; Hammer, *The Court-Martial of Lt. Calley,* 328–33, 344–48; Belknap, *The Vietnam War on Trial,* 183–84.

39. "Calley Case Goes to Military Jury," *New York Times* (March 17, 1971): 1, 20; Hammer, *The Court-Martial of Lt. Calley,* 334–43; Belknap, *The Vietnam War on Trial,* 185.

40. "Calley Case Goes to Military Jury," *New York Times* (March 17, 1971): 1, 20; Hammer, *The Court-Martial of Lt. Calley,* 349–53; Belknap, *The Vietnam War on Trial,* 186–87.

41. "Calley Guilty of Murder of 22 Civilians at Mylai," *New York Times* (March 30, 1971): 1, 12; "Text of Calley Verdict," *New York Times* (March 30, 1971): 12; Colonel Reid W. Kennedy (USA, ret.), "My Lai / Trial of Lieutenant William Calley / A Soldier's Duty to say 'No,'" Lecture delivered at Washington and Lee University, October 23, 1985, transcript provided to the author by Colonel Raymond Ruhlmann (USMC, ret.).

42. "Calley Pleads for Understanding," *New York Times* (March 31, 1971): 1, 18; "Text of Calley Statement," *New York Times* (March 31, 1971): 18; Hammer, *The Court-Martial of Lt. Calley,* 354–68; Belknap, *The Vietnam War on Trial,* 189–90.

43. "Calley Sentenced to Life for Murders at Mylai 4," *New York Times* (April 1, 1971): 1, 18; Hammer, *The Court-Martial of Lt. Calley,* 368–69; Belknap, *The Vietnam War on Trial,* 190.

44. Calley Court-Martial Survey Results, "Famous American Trials: The My Lai Courts-Martial," University of Missouri at Kansas City Law School, http://law2.umkc.edu/faculty/projects/ftrials/mylai/SurveyResults.html, accessed December 13, 2010.

45. Belknap, *The Vietnam War on Trial,* 194–95.

46. "Decision by Nixon on Calley Hailed, Protests over Conviction Continue across Nation," *New York Times* (April 3, 1971): 14; "U.S. Command in Vietnam Bars 'Battle Hymn of Calley' from Radio Network, Citing Pending Appeal," *New York Times* (May 1, 1971): 4.

47. Rick Perlstein, *Nixonland: The Rise of a President and the Fracturing of America* (New York: Scribner, 2008), 555–56; Hammer, *The Court-Martial of Lieutenant Calley,* 379–81.

48. Aubrey M. Daniel to Richard M. Nixon, April 3, 1971, Document CK3100526876, Declassified Documents Reference System, Online, [accessed De-

cember 13, 2010]. The text of the letter is also available on the University of Missouri, Kansas City, Law School's Famous Trials: My Lai website at http://law2.umkc.edu/faculty/projects/ftrials/mylai/daniels_ltr.html [accessed November 28, 2011].

49. Michael Novak, "The Battle Hymn of Lt. Calley and the Republic," *Commonweal* (April 30, 1971): 183.

50. "Viewpoints on the Calley Trial," *Senior Scholastic* (May 10, 1971): 12–13.

51. "Judgment at Fort Benning," *New York Times* (March 30, 1971): 34.

52. Belknap, *The Vietnam War on Trial*, 192; "The Calley Verdict," *Chicago Tribune* (April 8, 1971): 20.

53. Perlstein, *Nixonland*, 557–66. For more on veterans' protests against the Vietnam War, see Richard Moser, *The New Winter Soldiers: GI and Veteran Dissent during the Vietnam Era* (New Brunswick, NJ: Rutgers University Press, 1996); Gary Kulik, *"War Stories": False Atrocity Tales, Swift Boaters, and Winter Soldiers—What Really Happened in Vietnam* (Washington, DC: Potomac, 2009); Richard Stacewicz, *Winter Soldiers: An Oral History of the Vietnam Veterans Against the War* (Chicago: Haymarket, 2008); and Andrew Hunt, *The Turning: A History of Vietnam Veterans Against the War* (New York: New York University Press, 2001).

54. United States v. Calley, CM 426402, US Army Court of Military Review, 46 CMR 1131; 1973 CMR Lexis 843; United States v. Calley, No. 26875, US Court of Military Appeals, 22 USCMA 534; 1973 CMA Lexis 627; 48 CMR 19; Calley v. Callaway, 382 F. Supp. 650 (1974), in Joseph Goldstein, Burke Marshall, and Jack Schwartz, eds., *The My Lai Massacre and Its Cover-Up: Beyond the Reach of the Law?* (New York: Free Press, 1976), 535–55; Calley v. Callaway, US Court of Appeals for Fifth Circuit, September 10, 1975, in Goldstein, Marshall, and Schwartz, *The My Lai Massacre and Its Cover-Up*, 556–73; Belknap, *The Vietnam War on Trial*, 235–54; Fact Sheet, Court-Martial of First Lieutenant William Calley, RG 319, Records Pertaining to Calley Court-Martial, Box 6, My Lai Lessons Learned Folder, NARA.

CHAPTER SIX: Responsibility

1. Michael Bilton and Kevin Sim, *Four Hours in My Lai* (New York: Viking, 1992), 348; Michal R. Belknap, *The Vietnam War on Trial: The My Lai Massacre and the Court-Martial of Lieutenant Calley* (Lawrence: University Press of Kansas, 2002), 228.

2. "Prosecution Says that Medina 'Chose Not to Intervene' at My Lai," *New York Times* (August 17, 1971): 8; US Army, Field Manual 27-10: *The Law of Land Warfare* (Washington, DC: Government Printing Office, 1956), 501; Belknap, *The Vietnam War on Trial*, 231–32.

3. David L. Anderson, ed., *Facing My Lai: Moving beyond the Massacre* (Lawrence: University Press of Kansas, 1998), 42–43.

4. "Nixon May Be Asked to Intervene in Medina Trial," *New York Times* (August 20, 1971): 8; "Medina Said to Have Felt He Lost Control of Troops," *New York Times* (August 27, 1971): 8.

5. "Witness Places Medina in Mylai," *New York Times* (August 25, 1971): 9; "Nine

Witnesses Unable to Place Medina at Site of Mylai Slayings," *New York Times* (August 18, 1971): 4.

6. "Medina Defends Action at Mylai," *New York Times* (September 17, 1971): 17; "Prosecution Says that Medina 'Chose Not to Intervene' at My Lai," *New York Times* (August 17, 1971): 8.

7. "Calley to Appear at Medina's Trial," *New York Times* (September 8, 1971): 17; "Calley May Balk at Medina Trial," *New York Times* (September 12, 1971): 13; "Medina Witness Admits Shooting Boy," *New York Times* (September 14, 1971): 12; Mary McCarthy, *Medina* (London: Wildwood House, 1972), 59–61.

8. "Witnesses Place Medina in Mylai," *New York Times* (August 25, 1971): 9; "Medina Witness Admits Shooting Boy," *New York Times* (September 14, 1971): 12; "A Medina Charge Reduced by Judge," *New York Times* (September 18, 1971): 1, 27.

9. "Army Withdraws Witness at Medina's Court-Martial," *New York Times* (August 26, 1971): 15; "Medina Case Witness Wins Plea on Contempt," *New York Times* (August 31, 1971): 10; McCarthy, *Medina*, 50–57.

10. "Judge Refuses to Dismiss Case against Medina in Mylai Deaths," *New York Times* (September 11, 1971): 11; "Medina Trial Told that Calley Said Killings Surprised Captain," *New York Times* (September 15, 1971): 14.

11. "Medina Defense Gains Two Points," *New York Times* (September 16, 1971): 6; McCarthy, *Medina*, 50.

12. "Judge Refuses to Dismiss Case against Medina in Mylai Deaths," *New York Times* (September 11, 1971): 11; "A Medina Charge Reduced by Judge," *New York Times* (September 18, 1971): 1, 27; Belknap, *The Vietnam War on Trial*, 230–31; McCarthy, *Medina*, 54–55.

13. "Medina Found Not Guilty of All Charges on Mylai," *New York Times* (September 23, 1971): 1, 26; McCarthy, *Medina*, 85–86; Belknap, *The Vietnam War on Trial*, 232.

14. Fact Sheet, Court-Martial of First Lieutenant William Calley, RG 319, Records of the Army Staff, Records Pertaining to Calley Court-Martial, Box 6, My Lai Lessons Learned Folder, NARA; "Trial Told Kotouc Maimed Prisoner," *New York Times* (April 27, 1971): 10; "Kotouc Is Acquitted of Maiming a Vietnamese Prisoner at Mylai," *New York Times* (April 30, 1971): 1, 5; Belknap, *The Vietnam War on Trial*, 227; Bilton and Sim, *Four Hours in My Lai*, 346–47.

15. "Army Inquiry Charges 14 Officers in Suppression of Songmy Facts," *New York Times* (March 18, 1970): 1, 14; Bilton and Sim, *Four Hours in My Lai*, 380–83.

16. "First Army's Chief Censures Gen. Koster in Mylai Incident," *New York Times* (January 31, 1971): 3; "General Demoted over Mylai Case," *New York Times* (May 20, 1971): 1, 9; Seymour Hersh, *Cover-Up: The Army's Secret Investigation of the Massacre at My Lai 4* (New York: Random House, 1972), 259–62; Bilton and Sim, *Four Hours in My Lai*, 326–28; Lewis Sorley, *Westmoreland: The General Who Lost Vietnam* (Boston: Houghton Mifflin Harcourt, 2011), 214.

17. "Court-Martial of Mylai Colonel Recessed after Jury Is Picked," *New York Times* (August 5, 1971): 6.

18. Luther C. West, *They Call It Justice: Command Influence and the Court-Martial System* (New York: Viking, 1977), 198–207.

19. "Lies about My Lai," *Time* (November 29, 1971): 31.

20. "Army Jury Gets Henderson Case," *New York Times* (December 17, 1971): 27; "Col. Henderson Acquitted in Last of the Mylai Cases," *New York Times* (December 18, 1971): 1, 16; West, *They Call It Justice,* 200–212; Hersh, *Cover-Up,* 265–68.

21. Lawrence Rockwood, *Walking Away from Nuremberg: Just War and the Doctrine of Command Responsibility* (Amherst: University of Massachusetts Press, 2007), 126.

22. Sorley, *Westmoreland,* 215–16.

23. Memorandum for the Secretary of the General Staff, "Lessons Learned from the Son My Incident," 15 June 1972, RG 319, Records Pertaining to Calley Court-Martial, Box 6, My Lai Lessons Learned Folder, NARA; Guenter Lewy, *America in Vietnam* (Oxford: Oxford University Press, 1978), 366–69; Frederic L. Borch, *Judge Advocates in Combat: Army Lawyers in Military Operations from Vietnam to Haiti* (Washington, DC: Office of the Judge Advocate General and US Army Center of Military History, 2001), 51–52.

24. Lewy, *America in Vietnam,* 153–61; Robert D. Heinl, "The Collapse of the Armed Forces," *Armed Forces Journal* 108, no. 19 (June 7, 1971): 30–38; Richard A. Gabriel and Paul L. Savage, *Crisis in Command: Mismanagement in the Army* (New York: Hill and Wang, 1978); William C. Westmoreland, *A Soldier Reports* (New York: Da Capo Press, 1989), 378.

25. Ronald H. Spector, *After Tet: The Bloodiest Year in Vietnam* (New York: Vintage, 1993), 26–38; Peter S. Kindsvatter, *American Soldiers: Ground Combat in the World Wars, Korea, and Vietnam* (Lawrence: University Press of Kansas, 2003), 229–45; Ron Milam, *Not a Gentleman's War: An Inside View of Junior Officers in the Vietnam War* (Chapel Hill: University of North Carolina Press, 2009), 162–64.

26. E. M. Barker, "Command Influence: Time for Revision?" *JAG Journal* 26, no. 1 (Fall 1971): 47–62; C. W. Corddry, "Jurisdiction to Try Discharged Servicemen for Violations of the Laws of War," *JAG Journal* 26, no. 1 (Fall 1971): 63–76; see War Crimes Act (1996), codified in US Code, Title 18 §2441.

27. Telford Taylor, *Nuremberg and Vietnam: An American Tragedy* (Chicago: Quadrangle, 1970); Rockwood, *Walking Away from Nuremberg,* 127–29.

28. Waldemar A. Solf, "A Response to Telford Taylor's *Nuremberg and Vietnam: An American Tragedy,*" *Akron Law Review* 5, no. 1 (Winter 1972): 43–68; W. Hays Parks, "Command Responsibility for War Crimes," *Military Law Review* 62 (Fall 1973): 1–104; Norman G. Cooper, "My Lai and Military Justice—To What Effect?" *Military Law Review* 59 (Winter 1973): 93–127; W. Hays Parks, "Crimes in Hostilities," *Marine Corps Gazette* 60, no. 9 (September 1976): 33–39; Gary D. Solis, "Obedience of Orders and the Law of War: Judicial Application in American Forums," *American University International Law Review* 15 (2000): 481–526.

Epilogue

1. Kendrick Oliver, “Coming to Terms with the Past: My Lai,” *History Today* 56, no. 2 (February 2006): 37–39; B. G. Burkett and Glenna Whitely, *Stolen Valor: How the Vietnam Generation Was Robbed of Its Heroes and Its History* (Dallas: Verity, 1998).

2. Kendrick Oliver, *The My Lai Massacre in American History and Memory* (Manchester, UK: Manchester University Press, 2006); Christian Appy, *Patriots: The Vietnam War Remembered from All Sides* (New York: Viking, 2003); Carol Becker, “Pilgrimage to My Lai: Social Memory and the Making of Art,” *Art Journal* (Winter 2003): 51–65.

3. Heonik Kwon, *After the Massacre: Commemoration and Consolation in Ha My and My Lai* (Berkeley: University of California Press, 2006); Nguyen-Vo Thu-Huong, “Forking Paths: How Shall We Mourn the Dead?” *Amerasia Journal* 31, no. 2 (2005): 157–75.

4. Oliver, *The My Lai Massacre in American History and Memory*, 274–81.

5. My Lai Peace Park, www.mylaipeacepark.org/peacepark_mylai.lasso (accessed December 2, 2011).

6. Deborah Nelson, *The War Behind Me: Vietnam Veterans Confront the Truth about U.S. War Crimes* (New York: Basic, 2008); Nick Turse, “Kill Anything that Moves: U.S. War Crimes and Atrocities, 1965–1973” (PhD diss., Columbia University, 2005); Frederic L. Borch, *Judge Advocates in Vietnam: Army Lawyers in Southeast Asia, 1959–1975* (Fort Leavenworth, KS: US Army Command and General Staff College Press, 2004), 34–35; Michael Sallah and Mitch Wiess, *Tiger Force: A True Story of Men and War* (Boston: Little, Brown, 2006).

7. Truda Gray and Brian Martin, “My Lai: The Struggle over Outrage,” *Peace and Change* 33, no. 1 (January 2008): 90–113; Daniel Ellsberg, “Counterinsurgency Tactics Led to Haditha, My Lai,” *New Perspectives Quarterly* 23, no. 3 (Summer 2006): 49–53; John M. Doris and Dominic Murphy, “From My Lai to Abu Ghraib: The Moral Psychology of Atrocity,” *Midwest Studies in Philosophy* 31 (2007): 25–55; Robert Jay Lifton, “Conditions of Atrocity,” *Nation* (May 31, 2004): 4–5; “Why Haditha Matters,” *Nation* (June 19, 2006): 4; Thomas E. Ricks, “In Haditha Killings, Details Come Slowly: Officer Version Is at Odds with Evidence,” *Washington Post* (June 4, 2006): A01; Seymour Hersh, “Chain of Command,” *New Yorker* 80, no. 12 (May 17, 2004): 38–43.

8. George S. Prugh, *Law at War: Vietnam, 1964–1973* (Washington, DC: Department of the Army, 1975), 114.

9. Richard Hammer, *The Court-Martial of Lieutenant Calley* (New York: Coward, McCann, & Geoghegan, 1971), 391.

10. Claude Cookman, “An American Atrocity: The My Lai Massacre Concretized in a Victim’s Face,” *Journal of American History* 94, no. 1 (June 2007): 154–62.

11. Kendrick Oliver, “Atrocity, Authenticity and American Exceptionalism: (Ir)rationalizing the Massacre at My Lai,” *Journal of American Studies* 37, no. 2 (2003): 268.

12. “William Calley Apologizes for My Lai Massacre,” Columbus, Georgia, *Ledger-Enquirer* (August 21, 2009): 1.

SUGGESTED FURTHER READING

The literature and primary source material on the Vietnam War is vast, if not overwhelming. A wealth of excellent sources on all aspects of the war, including My Lai, are readily available for student research. The listing below of selected primary and secondary materials used primarily in this volume serves as a guide for further inquiry into My Lai and related topics.

There are many valuable general histories of the American war in Vietnam. Among the more thorough but concise are George Herring, *America's Longest War: The United States and Vietnam, 1950–1975*, 4th ed. (Boston: McGraw-Hill, 2002); James S. Olson and Randy Roberts, *Where the Domino Fell: America and Vietnam, 1945–1995*, rev. 5th ed. (Malden, MA: Blackwell, 2008); Gary R. Hess, *Vietnam and the United States: Origins and Legacy of War*, rev. ed. (New York: Twayne, 1998); George Donelson Moss, *Vietnam: An American Ordeal*, 6th ed. (Upper Saddle River, NJ: Prentice Hall, 2010); Patrick J. Hearden, *The Tragedy of Vietnam*, 3rd ed. (New York: Pearson Longman, 2008); Andy Weist, *The Vietnam War, 1956–1975* (Oxford: Osprey, 2002); and David L. Anderson, *The Vietnam War* (New York: Palgrave Macmillan, 2005). More substantial works include Marilyn B. Young, *The Vietnam Wars, 1945–1990* (New York: Harper Collins, 1991); Robert Shulzinger, *A Time for War: The United States and Vietnam, 1941–1975* (New York: Oxford University Press, 1997); Phillip B. Davidson, *Vietnam at War: The History, 1946–1975* (New York: Oxford University Press, 1988); Frances FitzGerald, *Fire in the Lake: The Americans and the Vietnamese* (New York: Vintage, 1972); Stanley Karnow, *Vietnam: A History* (New York: Viking, 1983); and John Prados, *Vietnam: The History of an Unwinnable War, 1945–1975* (Lawrence: University Press of Kansas, 2009).

Several works deal with the combat experience of American soldiers in Vietnam, written by veterans and scholars. Among these many outstanding works are Philip Caputo, *A Rumor of War* (New York: Ballantine, 1977); James Ebert, *A Life in a Year: The American Infantryman in Vietnam, 1965–1972* (Novato, CA: Presidio Press, 1993); and Ronald H. Spector, *After Tet: The Bloodiest Year in Vietnam* (New York: Vintage, 1994). Broader histories of the soldier's experience in Vietnam include: Andrew Krepinevich, *The Army and Vietnam* (Baltimore: Johns Hopkins University Press, 1986); Christian Appy, *Working-Class War: American Combat Soldiers and Vietnam* (Chapel Hill: University of North Carolina Press, 1993); Gunter Lewy, *America in Vietnam* (New York: Oxford University Press, 1978); and James E. Westheider, *The Vietnam War* (Westport, CT: Greenwood, 2007). William A. Strauss examines the draft in *Chance and Circumstance: The Draft, the War, and the Vietnam Generation* (New York: Knopf, 1978), and Ron Milam counters the myth of the incompetent junior officer in *Not a Gentleman's War: An Inside View of Junior Officers in the Vietnam War* (Chapel Hill: University of North Carolina Press, 2009). For a comparative view of the soldier's experience, see Andrew J. Huebner, *The Warrior Image: Soldiers in American Culture from the Second World War to the Vietnam Era* (Chapel Hill: University of North Carolina Press, 2008); Peter S. Kindsvatter, *American Soldiers: Ground Combat in the World Wars, Korea, and Vietnam* (Lawrence: University Press of Kansas, 2003); and John C. McManus, *Grunts: Inside the American Infantry Combat Experience, World War II through Iraq* (New York: NAL Caliber, 2010).

For military justice issues, including war crimes, see Jonathan Lurie, *Military Justice in America: The U.S. Court of Appeals for the Armed Forces, 1775–1980* (Lawrence: University Press of Kansas, 2001); Mark J. Osiel, *Obeying Orders: Atrocity, Military Discipline, and the Law of War* (London: Transaction, 1999); and William Thomas Allison, *Military Justice in Vietnam: The Rule of Law in an American War* (Lawrence: University Press of Kansas, 2007). The study of war crimes in Vietnam remains contentious and provocative: see Deborah Nelson, *The War Behind Me: Vietnam Veterans Confront the Truth about U.S. War Crimes* (New York: Basic, 2008); Gary Kulik, *"War Stories": False Atrocity Tales, Swift Boaters, and Winter Soldiers—What Really Happened in Vietnam* (Washington, DC: Potomac, 2009); Bernd Greiner, *War without Fronts: The USA in Vietnam* (New Haven: Yale University Press, 2009); Nick Turse, "Kill Anything that Moves: U.S. War Crimes and Atrocities, 1965–1973" (PhD diss., Columbia University, 2005); and Richard Moser, *The New Winter Soldiers: GI and Veteran Dissent during the Vietnam Era* (New Brunswick, NJ: Rutgers University Press, 1996). Valuable official service histories include George S. Prugh, *Law at War: Vietnam, 1964–1973* (Washington, DC: Department of the Army, 1975); Gary Solis, *Marines and Military Law in Vietnam: Trial by Fire* (Washington, DC: USMC History and Museums Division, 1989); and Frederic L. Borch, *Judge Advocates in Combat: Army Lawyers in Military Operations from Vietnam to Haiti* (Washington, DC: Office of the Judge Advocate General and US Army Center of Military History, 2001). In addition to My Lai, other incidents involving American forces in Vietnam have received careful examination: see, for example, Michael Sallah and Mitch Wiess, *Tiger Force: A True Story of Men and War* (Boston: Little, Brown, 2006), and Gary D. Solis, *Son Thang: An American War Crime* (New York: Bantam, 1997).

Numerous journalists have examined various aspects of My Lai, including the investigations and courts-martial. Of the early groundbreaking work by journalists, see Seymour Hersh's *My Lai 4: A Report on the Massacre and Its Aftermath* (New York: Random House, 1970) and *Cover-Up: The Army's Secret Investigation of the Massacre at My Lai 4* (New York: Random House, 1972); Richard Hammer, *One Morning in the War: The Tragedy at Son My* (New York: Coward-McCann, 1970) and *The Court-Martial of Lt. Calley* (New York: Coward, McCann, & Geoghegan, 1971); Martin Gershen, *Destroy or Die: The True Story of My Lai* (New Rochelle, NY: Arlington House, 1971); Wayne Greenhaw, *The Making of a Hero: The Story of Lieut. William Calley Jr.* (Louisville, KY: Touchstone, 1971); Arthur Everett, Kathryn Johnson, and Harry F. Rosenthal, *Calley* (New York: Dell, 1971); Mary McCarthy, *Medina* (London: Wildwood House, 1972); and John Sack, *Lieutenant Calley: His Own Story* (New York: Grosset & Dunlap, 1970). A later and deeply detailed account of the actual massacre is Michael Bilton and Kevin Sim, *Four Hours in My Lai* (New York: Penguin, 1992). Trent Angers told Hugh Thompson's story in his *The Forgotten Hero of My Lai: The Hugh Thompson Story* (Lafayette, LA: Acadian House, 1999). On media reporting of My Lai, see William G. Hammond, *Reporting Vietnam: Media and Military at War* (Lawrence: University Press of Kansas, 1998).

Some participants in the investigations and trials have written about their experiences. William V. Wilson, who participated in both the Army CID and Peers Inquiry investigations, offered his experiences in "I Had Prayed to God that This Thing Was Fiction," *American Heritage* (February 1990): 44–53, and William R. Peers, who led the Army investigation into the cover-up, described his experience in *The My Lai Inquiry* (New York: Norton, 1979). Ron Ridenhour offered his story of slowly realizing what happened at My Lai in "Heroes at the Massacre," *Playboy* (March 1993): 88, and William G. Eckhardt, the Army's lead prosecutor in several of the trials, recounted his view of My Lai and the subsequent courts-martial in "My Lai: An American Tragedy," *UMKC Law Review* 68 (Summer 2000): 671–703.

Scholars continue to explore all aspects of My Lai. For an excellent discussion of the Calley court-martial, see Michal R. Belknap, *The Vietnam War on Trial: The My Lai Massacre and the Court-Martial of Lieutenant William Calley* (Lawrence: University Press of Kansas, 2002). David L. Anderson's edited proceedings of a conference on My Lai held at Tulane University in 1994, *Facing My Lai: Moving beyond the Massacre* (Lawrence: University Press of Kansas, 1998), includes illuminating discussion among scholars and some of the men involved in the My Lai story, including William G. Eckhardt, Ron Ridenhour, and Hugh Thompson. Recent scholars have also used memory as a framework to examine My Lai and its long-term impact on both American and Vietnamese societies. Kendrick Oliver's *The My Lai Massacre in American History and Memory* (Manchester, UK: Manchester University Press, 2006) and Heonik Kwon's *After the Massacre: Commemoration and Consolation in Ha My and My Lai* (Berkeley: University of California Press, 2006) offer insightful examinations of My Lai utilizing these fresh and revealing historical approaches. For a succinct overview of My Lai, see James S. Olson and Randy Roberts, *My Lai: A Brief History with Documents* (Boston: Bedford, 1998).

Primary material on My Lai is both immense and accessible. Among the several Vietnam-related record groups at the National Archives and Records Administration in College Park, MD, Record Group 472, Records of US Forces in Southeast Asia; Record Group 153, Records of the Office of the Judge Advocate General (Army); Record Group 335, Records of the Office of the Secretary of the Army; Record Group 319, Records of the Army Staff; and the Nixon Papers contain resources on My Lai, the investigations, and particularly the Calley court-martial.

The Peers Inquiry report's first volume is reprinted, along with several other documents and case rulings, in Joseph Goldstein, Burke Marshall, and Jack Schwartz, *The My Lai Massacre and Its Cover-Up: Beyond the Reach of the Law?* (New York: Free Press, 1976). The entire Peers Inquiry report, *Report of the Department of the Army Review of the Preliminary Investigations into the My Lai Incident* (Washington, DC: Department of the Army, 1970), is available through the National Archives and Records Administration, government depository libraries, and online at the Library of Congress (www.loc.gov/rr/frd/Military_Law/Peers_inquiry.html), among other sites. Robert Lester's *The Peers Inquiry of the Massacre at My Lai* (Bethesda, MD: University Publications of America, 1997) is the guide to the National Archives and Records Administration microfilm of the entire Peers Inquiry report.

The congressional investigation of My Lai is printed as *Report of the Armed Services Investigating Subcommittee of the Committee on Armed Services, 91st Congress, House of Representatives, 2nd Session, July 15, 1970* (Washington, DC: Government Printing Office, 1970). Mark D. Carson's "F. Edward Hébert and the Congressional Investigation of the My Lai Massacre," *Louisiana History* 37, no. 1 (Winter 1996): 61–79, provides context for the congressional investigation. Additionally, the Vietnam Center at Texas Tech University contains an enormous archive of My Lai–related materials, including investigation reports, witness statements, and other sources, much of which has been digitized and is available online at www.vietnam.ttu.edu. Another excellent online resource for My Lai is the University of Missouri–Kansas City, Law School's "Great Trials" section on My Lai and the Calley court-martial at http://law2.umkc.edu/faculty/projects/ftrials/mylai/mylai.htm.

Additionally, several periodicals and newspapers from 1968 through the early 1970s offered excellent coverage and insight as the investigations and trials unfolded. Among others, the *New York Times* followed the Calley trial daily. *Life, Time, Newsweek,* and others provided near constant coverage once the incident became known to the public in 1969. Editorials and other essays in the *Nation,* the *New Republic,* and *Commonweal,* among others, offer insight into public and "talking head" reaction to the incident and the trials, especially the Calley verdict. Gallup and Harris poll data are also easily accessible.

INDEX